# THE WORLD ON OUR DOORSTEP

## EVANGELICAL MISSION AND OTHER FAITHS

# DEWI HUGHES

evangelical alliance
better together

NOVEMBER 2016

First published in Great Britain 2016
Evangelical Alliance
176 Copenhagen Street
London
N1 0ST

The author and publisher have made every effort to ensure the accuracy of
external websites, email addresses and resource suggestions including
in this book. Neither the author nor publisher are responsible for the
content or continued availability of these sites and resources.

ISBN 978-0-9572448-2-5

The Evangelical Alliance is a company limited by guarantee,
registered in England & Wales No. 123448.
Registered Charity No England and Wales: 212325, Scotland: SC040576.

# www.eauk.org

# Contents

# Acknowledgements

Without a lot of help from many friends this resource would not have been written:

I spent but a short time with Kevin Sadler in his church building in Birmingham. In that short time I gained invaluable insight, which I could not have gained in any other way, into what it means to serve Jesus faithfully in the overwhelming and sometimes explicitly hostile presence of one of the religions.

Don Horrocks was responsible for getting me going with the project. He put a lot of effort into putting me on the right track spiced by enjoyable walks in the Welsh hills. He retired from the Alliance during the project, but continued to read drafts, comment and encourage.

Robin Thomson of South Asian Concern shared a lot of material with me that provided the backbone for the chapters on reaching adherents of the other religions and caring for them when they become disciples of Jesus. He also commented in great detail on a full draft. His comments were invariably helpful and have made this resource much better than it would otherwise have been.

Kate Wharton wrote a paper on caring for converts from the religions while working as an advisor on the religions at

Lambeth Palace during Rowan Williams' time as archbishop. This was used extensively in the chapter on caring for those that have become disciples of Jesus.

The resource comes out of what is now called the Evangelical Alliance's Theological Advisory Group. Many commented on drafts. Three members have been particularly helpful – Rose Dowsett, Dan Strange and Jenny Taylor.

The work done by Ann Bower of Global Connections that is now visible in the 'Mission Issues' page of their website was ready with her encouragement.

For the chapter on 'Dialogue' I received invaluable help from Imtiaz Khan of London City Mission's Ley Street Mission in Ilford and Tom Wilson of St Philip's Centre, Leicester.

Trevor Cooling found time in a very busy schedule to point me in the right direction on many issues in the chapter on 'Education'.

Jim Stewart from the Evangelical Alliance Wales office provided material and insight for the chapter on 'Politics'.

The text was skilfully prepared for printing by Daniel Webster and other members of the Evangelical Alliance staff. I'm very grateful that they bore more of this burden than would normally be expected because of the health issues that I was facing at the time.

I want to express my gratitude to all these friends that contributed so generously to the process of making this resource what it is. That said, final responsibility for this resource is mine - warts and all.

# Foreword
## Steve Clifford, general director, Evangelical Alliance

A few years ago I was at a civic gathering, with local politicians and leaders from different faith groups. When it was my turn to speak I made a point of emphasising that I was committed to my faith, which hopefully was not a surprise. I went on to say that part of that commitment was passionately wanting other people, including those from other faiths, to become followers of Christ. I unashamedly stated that the Christian faith is a pros-elytising faith – this is something we are to have confidence in – and I would attempt to persuade them of the truth and goodness of Christianity. The other side of this, and this I made clear, is that I wanted them to be free to try and persuade me of their religious beliefs. This is what religious freedom is all about, we contend for the right of all people to hear the good news of Jesus Christ, and to have the freedom to accept or reject that message.

The Good News is at the heart of the Evangelical Alliance and we are committed to helping the Church in the UK keep it central to its work. Introducing people to the good news of Jesus and discovering saving faith has to be core business to the church.

This mission has taken Christians to every corner of the globe. The missionary endeavours of previous generations took the message of Jesus – often at significant personal cost – to places where His name had not been heard, to people from major religions and innumerable belief systems.

The zeal of foreign mission certainly was not without its flaws and its legacy is complicated – often infused with Western cultural practices as much as the transforming message of Jesus. It was also the practice of relatively few Christians, who would often buy a one-way ticket to untraveled lands.

We live in a different world today. Not only is travel much easier, and the task of overseas mission practically less challenging – although there remain places where to speak of Jesus's good news places the bearer of that message in considerable peril – our neighbours are often from the places our ancestors took their missionary message. The world is on our doorstep.

This has meant that some of our most passionate churches in the UK are from the places missionaries planted the seed of the gospel, and their role in proclaiming Jesus' name in our communities provides a much-needed infusion of energy and belief into our society that might otherwise find it even easier to sideline God from day-to-day life.

In other ways religious belief is also harder to ignore. We are used to seeing mosques, temples and gurdwaras in our neighbourhoods, and the impact of belief on global politics has rarely been more central. Despite the fervent wishes of some, our society is catching up with the rest of the world, and religion is becoming more important.

The task in front of us as we talk about Jesus and encourage people to place their faith in him cannot be detached from engaging with people from the religions. It is not enough to reach out to those who have no or little belief (although that is essential), we must introduce people to Jesus who have never thought that learning of his life and message, and believing in his death and resurrection, could have any meaning to them.

In this book Dewi Hughes helpfully outlines the intricacies involved in mission towards people of other religious faiths. Through looking at theological, pastoral and cultural issues involved he provokes us to a fresh missionary effort. Growing up I heard about Hudson Taylor, Jim and Elizabeth Elliot, and countless others who were heroes of our faith. I look forward to sharing stories of new heroes who commit their lives to telling their neighbours from diverse beliefs and backgrounds that Jesus's good news is for them, and trusting in him brings salvation and abundant life.

It is time for us to reach the world on our doorstep.

# INTRODUCTION:
# Religions in the UK

The religious scene in the UK has changed significantly since the Evangelical Alliance published *Christianity and other Faiths; An Evangelical Contribution to our Multi-Faith Society* in 1983.[1] All the world religions that were already well-established by the 1970s have grown in numbers, profile and confidence since then. It is now impossible to ignore them. To be serious about our call to mission as evangelicals in the UK we must be serious about these religions. This is particularly the case in many cities where adherents now represent a significant proportion of the population.

The 'religion' question in the 2011 Census means that we have extensive knowledge of the location of adherents of different religions across the UK, and in Chapter 1 we will look at some of the changing profiles and where the greatest concentrations lie.

The purpose of this volume is to:

1  Awaken evangelicals to this reality and to point to resources that will help in gaining an understanding of the religions.

---

1  Exeter: Paternoster Press, 1983. *Christianity and other Faiths* was a booklet in three parts that focused on 1) the status of other faiths, 2) Christian attitudes and action and 3) practical problems. Much of the material remains relevant and useful today.

2 Look at recent developments in missionary thinking that will help in formulating a mission strategy.

3 Examine various approaches to evangelism.

4 Explore some of the pastoral issues that arise from ministering to people of other religions.

5 Consider the ramifications for education and politics.

The religions that are in focus are what are often called the world religions: Buddhism, Hinduism, Islam, Judaism and Sikhism. Religion is clearly a slippery and subjective word. Conceptually, it covers a variety of spiritual categories such as worship, faith and belief. Although it may provide a handy way to characterise the subject matter of this resource, it needs to be acknowledged that it is also insufficient in as much as it can never fully convey the substance of belief. Being written from an evangelical perspective, this insufficiency is especially marked in relation to a stream of the Christian faith in which observable 'religious' rites and rituals are often notable by their absence. This volume does not address Judaism in detail, the imperative towards mission is the same, but many of the cultural, theological and surrounding issues differ.

In Britain today even if the number of people identifying as Christians has dipped below half[2], it is still a significant factor in many aspects of public and community life. For evangelical Christians, the number of whom is around three to four per cent of the population, they too could be considered a minority religion.

The aim is not to provide an exhaustive treatment of any topic but an accessible guide to the main issues with information about resources that will enable deeper consideration. It is also recognised that there is a range of evangelical views on many

2 British Social Attitudes 28 (NatCen, 2012) p173
  http://www.bsa.natcen.ac.uk/media/38966/bsa28-full-report.pdf

issues. An attempt has been made to reflect this diversity. The overriding aim is to stir up evangelicals to reach out in love with the gospel of Jesus the Messiah to adherents of other religions.

Much has changed since 1980:

# The worldwide revival of religion

In 1980 the worldwide revival of the religions was gathering momentum. In 1979 Iran's westernising Shah was forced to flee and an Islamic Republic under the leadership of the Ayatollah Khomeini, a Muslim cleric, was established. In 1980 the nationalist movement in India united to form the BJP, a political party that is currently in power and has held power on a number of occasions since its foundation. One of its fundamental tenets is that India is a Hindu nation and should remain so. It has inspired legislation against conversion in a number of Indian states. Also in India in the early 1980s, the movement for the unification of Sikh land under Sikh authority was gathering momentum. This led to the storming of the sacred Golden Temple in Amritsar commanded by Indira Gandhi in June 1984 resulting in her assassination in the same year. In 1983 tensions between the Tamils and Sinhalese in Sri Lanka exploded in a bloody conflict that lasted for decades. The growth of Buddhist nationalism was an important contributory factor in the conflict, though cultural and social factors were also significant.

All these developments testify to a renewed confidence among many adherents of the religions in the post-colonial world of the second half of the 20th century. With many immigrants in the UK from countries where this religious revival was happening keeping up links with their countries of origin and fresh immigrants also arriving from those countries, it is inevitable that the effects of this revival should be felt in the UK. One obvious result is that adherents have become more devout, active and intolerant of others.

This new assertiveness may have been partly shaped by the colonial past of the countries where the world religions are dominant. This is particularly the case for the children and grandchildren of migrants. The original migrants were glad of the opportunity for a better life that migration gave them. Because many found themselves marginalised and subject to racist abuse, their children and grandchildren focus on the injustice of their colonial past and disadvantaged present. They look back to the pre-colonial era when their religious tradition dominated their culture. Many have come to see the colonial period as a period when their culture, which includes their religion, was humiliated by the Western empires. For some, they are now asserting their identity but because they are doing it in response to what is perceived as humiliation their assertiveness is sometimes expressed in the language of victimisation.

*Christianity and Other Faiths* was published in 1983, six years before the invention of the world wide web. This great revolution in the way in which people communicate has had a huge impact on the world of the religions. It has meant an immense loss of power and influence for the guardians of religious traditions, such as family and clergy. People with access to the internet can be influenced by all manner of religious movements. It has been very significant for a younger and educated generation that have plugged in to international movements that emanate from very different contexts and are far more negative about the context in which the second and third generations have been raised.

This revival of the religions has confounded the secularisation model that was still dominant in intellectual circles in the UK in 1980. Secularisation is the belief that religion will inevitably lose social significance in an urban, industrialised, westernised society. The undisputed decline of the churches in the UK in the second half of the 20th century bolstered the secular case and justified the marginalisation of Christians in the public square. But as formal Christianity has continued to decline since 1980, devout Christianity has continued to grow in parallel with the growth of devotion in the religions. Evangelical churches, especially those that are Charismatic or Pentecostal, are at the forefront of this growth, with black majority churches representing a very significant proportion of this growth. The result of this religious revival, Christian or otherwise, is that it has become much more difficult to ignore the significance of religion in public life.

## Outline of contents

This resource will look first to provide an overview of the state of minority religions in the UK in chapter 1. It will then consider the biblical, theological and missiological response to the religions, focusing particularly on idolatry and contextualisation (chapter 2). Chapter 3 examines some of the key principles of evangelism and their outworking in various contexts. Chapter 4 considers the pastoral issues that arise in caring for new believers with backgrounds in the religions. Chapter 5 describes three types of formal dialogue: apologetic/polemic, scriptural reasoning and building mutual understanding. It is argued that all three types can be the context for authentic witness. Chapter 6 looks at the ramifications of the intensified presence of the religions for education and the final chapter (chapter 7) examines the ramifications in the realm of politics. The underlying concern throughout the volume is for an authentic evangelical witness to the gospel to adherents of the religions.

# CHAPTER 1:
# Overview of religions

## Where adherents are concentrated

In 1980 the pattern was already well established for adherents of the religions to be concentrated in certain areas as well as scattered throughout the UK. This pattern has been significantly intensified since then. We also have much better knowledge of the location of adherents of the religions now because since 2001 government has taken much more interest in gathering information on adherents of the religions. There was a question on religious affiliation in the 2001 Census but it was the terrorist attacks of 9/11 and 7/7 that awakened government to be really serious about its gathering of data on religious affiliation. So, in the 2011 Census all residents in England and Wales were asked to which religion they belonged. The options available were Christian, Buddhist, Hindu, Jewish, Muslim, Sikh, and No Religion.[1] It was also possible to state affiliation to a religion other than the six that were stipulated. In the statistics that were eventually announced the percentage of those that did not tick

---

1   It should be noted that some Hindus, Sikhs and Muslims believe that their communities are much larger than suggested by the census

any box was also included. The results were published as numbers and percentages of the population of regions, counties, London boroughs, unitary authorities and districts in England and unitary authorities in Wales. The figures below are derived from data published by the Office of National Statistics[2].

# Muslims

2,706,066, which was 4.8% of the total population. This compares with the estimated figure of 553,000 in 1981, which was 1.1% of the total population.

This Muslim population is widely scattered through England and Wales:

- Over 90 local government areas are 1-4% Muslim
- Over 30 are 5-9% Muslim
- 26 are 10-19% Muslim
- That means that there are around 150 local government areas where between 1 and 19 in every hundred of the population is Muslim.
- About 25% of the population of Blackburn with Darwen, Bradford, Birmingham, Luton, Slough, Redbridge and Waltham Forest are Muslim
- About a third of the population of the London boroughs of Newham [32%] and Tower Hamlets [34.5%] are Muslim
- 37% of Muslims [1,012,823] live in Greater London amounting to 14.4% of the population of inner and 11.1% of outer London.

--------------------------------------------------------------

2   The statistics in this section are based on the report of the response
    to the religion question in the 2011census published by the Office of
    National Statistics - http://www.ons.gov.uk/ons/rel/census/2011-census/
    key-statistics-for-local-authorities-in-england-and-wales/rpt-religion.html

# Hindus

There were 816,633 Hindus, representing 1.5% of the total population of England and Wales. In 1981 there was an estimated 278,000 Hindus.

- Around 80 local government areas are between 1 and 4% Hindu
- 8 are between 5% and 9% Hindu
- 4 are between 10% and 19% Hindu
- Harrow is the only area over 20% with 25.3% [60,407] of the population Hindu. Leicester unitary authority [15.3% - 50,087] is the other area where Hindus are most concentrated.
- Almost 42% [341,113] of Hindus in England and Wales live in outer London with the greatest concentration in Barnet, Brent [55,449], Croydon, Ealing, Harrow [60,407], Hillingdon, Hounslow and Redbridge [31,699].

# Sikh

423,158 representing 0.8% of the total population of England and Wales. This compares with an estimated 144,000 in 1981. Sikh leaders believe that there are more Sikhs in the UK and that this would have been manifested if 'Sikh' had been included as an option in the ethnicity section of the census. But the census figure gives a clear picture of people's own perception of what religion they belong to.

- The Sikhs are not as widely spread in England and Wales as Muslims and Hindus and Slough is the only place where they are more than 10% of the population [10.6%].
- Though nowhere a very high proportion of the population, around a quarter of all Sikhs live in the

West Midlands Metropolitan County, [117,000 with concentrations in Birmingham – 32,000, Coventry – 16,000, Sandwell – 27,000, Walsall – 11,500 and Wolverhampton – 22,500], and another quarter live in outer London, [111,500 with concentrations in Ealing – 27,000, Hounslow – 23,000, Hillingdon - 18,000 and Redbridge – 17,000]. There are also significant concentrations of Sikhs in the Leicester unitary authority [14,500] West Yorkshire Metropolitan County [18,000 with 9,000 in Leeds and 5,000 in Bradford], and Gravesham, Kent [8,000].

- Around 30 local authority areas are between 1 and 4% Sikh.

# Jewish

There were 263,346 Jews in England and Wales according to the 2011 census. This was 0.5 per cent of the population. This meant that after years of decline, the Jewish community increased marginally from 259,927 in the 2001 census.

- Jews are scattered throughout the UK but normally in small numbers.

- There are significant Jewish populations in northern cities such as Gateshead [1.5% - 3000] and Greater Manchester [Bury 5.6% - 10,000; Salford 3.3% - 7,500] but the majority of Jews [56% - 148,602] are in Greater London. Over a third of London's Jews live in the borough of Barnet [54,084], accounting for one in five [20.5%] of all Jews in England and Wales.

- According to the Board of Deputies of British Jews the number of mainstream Jews is continuing to decline and that the ultra Orthodox is responsible for any growth.[3]

3   Additional information on British Jews comes from the website of the Board of Deputies of British Jews https://www.bod.org.uk/jewish-facts-info/jews-in-numbers/ (accessed 10/10/2016)

# Buddhist

247,743 said that they were Buddhist in the 2011 census. Buddhists are thinly scattered throughout England and Wales.

- There are 23 local authority areas that have more than 1% Buddhists in the population and 19 of these are in Greater London.
- In fact 33% of all Buddhists are in London [86,026 – Inner London 36,860; Outer London – 45,166].
- There are just two areas where more than 2% of the population are Buddhist – Lewisham [2.4%] and Rushmore, Hampshire [3.3%].
- The local authority areas with the largest number of Buddhists are all outer London boroughs – Barnet [4521], Brent [4300], Ealing [4228] and Greenwich [4223]. [4]

Christians were still in the majority in every local authority except Tower Hamlets in 2011 with 59.3% of the population of England and Wales stating that they are Christians. Even in Bradford, on paper at least, Christians outnumber Muslims by almost 2 to 1. Tower Hamlets is the only borough where Muslims [34.5%] outnumber Christians [27.1%]. But there are some authorities that have become thoroughly pluralist. In Leicester Unitary Authority Hindus, Muslims and Sikhs together [38.2%] outnumber Christians [32.4%]. Harrow is the most plural borough in England and Wales – Christian [37%], Buddhist [1.1%], Hindu [25.3%], Jewish [4.4%], Muslim [12.5%], Sikh [1.2%], other religions [2.5%]. Every religion is represented in Harrow in significant numbers and

---

4   Figures for faith groups in London are helpfully summarised in 'Assessment of GLA's impact on faith equality' p17 https://www.london.gov.uk/sites/default/files/assessment_of_the_glas_impact_on_faith_equality.pdf (accessed 31 October 2016)

adherents of religions other than Christianity make up 47% of the population. In Harrow those of no religion are only 9.6% as compared to the national average of 24.7%.

In the local authorities that have a high percentage of Muslims there are areas that are overwhelmingly Muslim. This is true, for example, in parts of Bradford, Birmingham and Tower Hamlets and Newham in London. From a mission perspective such areas benefit from an approach similar to that used in Muslim majority countries.

# Scotland

Although the percentage of adherents of the world religions is much smaller in Scotland, the pattern of significant increase between the censuses of 2001 and 2011 is the same. In 2011 Muslims represented 1.4% of the total population – up from 43,000 to 77,000, an increase of 34,000. They are concentrated in large urban areas, especially Glasgow, East Renfrewshire, Edinburgh, Dundee and Aberdeen City.

Although there are twice as many Muslims as Hindus, Sikhs and Buddhists added together these religions have also seen a significant increase in numbers between the two censuses. The Hindus have more than doubled in numbers with an increase of 10,000 – from 6,000 to 16,000. Together they represent 0.7% of the population of Scotland.[5]

# Northern Ireland[6]

Concentrated in Belfast the Muslim population of Northern Ireland also increased between 2001 and 2011. It went up from

5   For a helpful chart see http://www.scotlandscensus.gov.uk/documents/censusresults/release2a/StatsBulletin2A.pdf

6   For a general report see http://www.ninis2.nisra.gov.uk/public/census2011analysis/religion/religionCommentary.pdf

1,943 to 3,832. The 2011 figure represents just 0.21% of the population.

The number of Hindus more than doubled in the same period to 2,382, which represents 0.13% of the population.

## Wales

In Wales there were almost 46,000 Muslims representing 1.5% of the population – that is very similar to the percentage in Scotland. Half were resident in Cardiff [23,000]. Newport and Swansea were the only other areas with significant concentrations. As in Scotland there are twice as many Muslims as Hindus [10,000], Buddhists [9000] and Sikhs [3000] added together.

## Reasons for the numerical growth

The religions have grown numerically since 1980 for a number of reasons:

a) Immigration that continued apace especially during the 80s and 90s. This is particularly true of Muslims of which only 47% had been born in the UK according to the 2011 Census;

b) A birth rate that is higher than the general population. It is easy to assume that adherents of some religions such as Haredi Jews and some Muslims have large families but there is also some hard evidence that this is the case.[7]

c) Conversion. This is true of the missionary religions such as Islam and Buddhism. The most optimistic number of Muslim converts in the UK is around 100,000 that represent 3.7% of Muslims in England and Wales.[8]

--------

7   N.Tromans, E.Natamba, J.Jeffries, *Have women born outside the UK driven the rise in UK births since 2011?*, ONS, 2007

8   This is in a report commissioned by Faith Matters in 2010 – M.A.Kevin Brice, *A minority within a minority: a report on converts to Islam in the UK*, Faith Matters 2011.

d) A greater willingness to self-identify as a member of a religion resulting from the general revival of religions in the last quarter of the 20th century.

## Greater visibility

The religions have also become more visible to the general population; especially in areas where adherents are concentrated.

The most obvious manifestation of this is the increase in the number of religious buildings that obviously belong to the religions. Many mosques, Hindu temples and Sikh gurdwaras are hidden behind nondescript facades but there are many that are purpose-built and proclaim loudly the presence of the religion they represent. The first purpose-built Hindu temple was formally opened in Slough in 1981and many others have been opened since, such as the Shree Sanatan Hindu Mandir in Wembley, London, or the Shri Swaminarayan Mandir in Neasden, London.

There were an estimated 150 mosques in the UK in 1980. It is now estimated that there are more than 1,500. Many are purpose-built mosques that can accommodate large numbers of worshippers. Some, such as the Birmingham central Mosque and the London Central Mosque in Regent's Park were built in the 1970s but many more have been built since then. The Suffa-tul-Islam Central Masjid in Bradford is the largest purpose-built mosque in the UK and can accommodate 8,000 worshippers. As an impressive religious building it stands shoulder to shoulder with many cathedrals. There are now more than 30 mosques in England that can accommodate at least 3,000 worshippers. The Sikhs have also been building new gurdwaras. In 2003 Prince Charles opened the new building of the Sikh Gurdwara in Southall, London, which is the largest gurdwara outside India.

Dress is an aspect of culture but it can also be an indicator of religion. The most obvious change in the last 30 years is the massive increase in the number of veiled Muslim women seen out and about in towns and cities – many fully covered except for their eyes.[9] These women are the most visible image of the Muslim revival of strict adherence to a Saudi Arabian dress code and their increasing numbers.

The religions have also become far more visible in the media. Here again it is Islam that is most often in the news because of the actions of adherents that are involved with expressions of the religion which advocate violence to further its ends. After the horror of 9/11 in New York, the London bombings of 7 July 2005 proved beyond doubt that the Muslim community in the UK also had its radical and violent adherents. The constant attention given to young men and women from the UK that have gone to join the fight against President Assad in Syria in the name of *jihad* [effort/struggle] and latterly to join IS has kept a violent and deeply intolerant image of Muslims in the public eye. The mistrust and even fear of Muslims that such coverage could and does generate is a constant challenge to Christian love.

## Diversity within the religions – Buddhism and Islam

Except for Sikhs, where the ethnicity-religion relationship is very close, the religions are not monolithic bodies but divided by ethnicity, belief and practice. A brief survey of Buddhist and Muslim diversity will serve to illustrate this fact.

----

9   A fully covered Muslim woman wears the *hijab* – a veil that covers the head and chest – and the *niqab* – a veil that covers the face except for the eyes.

*Buddhism*
The three main branches of the Buddhist tradition[10] are well represented in the UK – and the three main branches have developed a bewildering variety of sub-branches. What follows gives a taste of the variety of Buddhist options that are now available in the UK. Almost all the centres and groups referred to have been established since 1980.

Southern Buddhism gained a foothold in the UK early in the 20th century coming from Sri Lanka via the Theosophical Society. Currently missionary monks have established a number of temples/meditation centres such as the Thai Amaravati Buddhist Monastery in Hertfordshire, the Sri Lankan Jethavana Buddhist Temple in Birmingham and the Burmese Saraniya Dhamma Meditation Centre in Salford.

Zen is the best-known Eastern Buddhist movement. This Japanese movement that originated in China has two main branches. The International Zen Association UK, which represents the Soto branch, has 15 meditation centres. Shobo-an in London and Fairlight in Luton are Rinzai Zen centres established by Christmas Humphries. Zen Yoga in Camberwell is also a Rinzai centre. The London Zen Centre in Crouch Hill, London, is affiliated to the Korean Kwan Um school of Zen.

The Northern Buddhist tradition has spread to the West as a result of the exile of Tibetan Buddhists under pressure from the Chinese Communist regime that has ruled Tibet since 1951. The Dalai Lama is the best-known Tibetan Buddhist leader in the West and he represents the Gelug [Yellow Hat]

---

10 This is a popular way of describing the Buddhist tradition among Western scholars.

tradition. The Lam Rim Buddhist centre in Raglan, Monmouth-shire and the Cham Tse Ling Buddhist Group in Preston belong to this tradition. The Kagyu [Black Hat] tradition is represented by the 17 Diamond Way centres in England and Scotland with the London Centre now at what used to be the Beaufoy Insti-tute in Lambeth. There are centres representing the Sakya [Red Hat] branch in Reading, Bristol and Bournemouth and the Bonpo have centres in London, Avebury, Glasgow and Swansea. The Buddhist penetration of the UK began as an import by intellectuals during the colonial era but it is now a vigorous missionary movement driven by Eastern monks and their Western converts.

*Islam*
The Muslim community also has many divisions where ethnicity and country of origin is even more significant than among Bud-dhists. With almost 44% of the Muslim population of England and Wales originating in Pakistan, "it is Pakistanis ... who tend to shape the public profile of Islam in Britain".[11] That does not mean that the Pakistani profile is uniform. In fact it reflects the development of Islamic factions in colonial India before the partition of India into Hindu and Muslim majority states. The two major factions of Islam generally are Sunni [90%] and Shi'a [10%]. Muslims of Pakistani origin in the UK are overwhelmingly Sunni and reflect the factions that emerged in India in the 20th century. The two main factions are focused on two universities/ seminaries in the Hanafi tradition of Muslim law. The largest faction is the Deobandi, named after the famous university/

---

11  Philip Lewis, 'Making Sense of Muslim Communities in Britain' in S.Bell and C. Chapman, *Between Naivety and Hostility; Uncovering the best Chris-tian responses to Islam in Britain*, Milton Keynes, Authentic, 2011, p. 83

seminary in Deoband, Uttar Pradesh, India.[12] According to the UK mosque statistics published in October 2014 on the Muslims in Britain website, 754 mosques representing 43.3% of the total number of mosques, are Deobandi. The second largest faction is the Bareilvi. This is a movement founded early in the 20th century by Raza Khan from the city of Bareilly in Uttar Pradesh, India, and is deeply influenced by the Indian mystical Muslim tradition [Sufism]. In the list referred to above 419 mosques are affiliated to the Bareilvi representing 24.1% of the total.

Historically these two movements were deeply antagonistic towards each other and spawned very different political movements in the struggle for Indian independence. The Deobandis supported the establishment of a united India as a secular state while the Bareilvis were opposed to Gandhi and supported the division of India into Muslim [Pakistan] and Hindu states.

More than two thirds of all mosques are either Deobandi or Bareilvi. The remaining third is shared between a number of affiliations the largest of which is the Salafi – 121 mosques - representing 7% of the total. Salafism is a movement originating in Saudi Arabia that advocates a return to the teaching and practice of the first four generations of Muslims – including Muhammad. It is a diverse movement advocating views ranging from a political focus on being good Muslims through peaceful engagement in the political process to violent jihad. One study of the movement has concluded that the quietist form of the movement was almost exclusively a European phenomenon.[13]

---

12  It is claimed that its reputation made it 2nd to Al-Azhar University in Egypt as a centre of Islamic learning.

13  Nicolet Boekhoff-van der Voort, Kees Versteegh and Joas Wagemakers, eds., *The Transmission and Dynamics of the Textual Sources of Islam: Essays in Honour of Harald Motzki*, Leiden, Brill, 2011, p.382

According to the 'Muslims in Britain list there are also eight [0.5%] mosques affiliated to the Muslim Brotherhood [Ikhwaan] – a revivalist and anti-imperialist movement that began in Egypt in the 1920s that was very influential in Egypt until its suppression in 2013.[14]

Some 71 mosques are Shia [4.1%]. The Shia became a separate form of Islam early in the history of the religion as a result of conflict over the leadership of the movement. Shias look to charismatic leaders to guide adherents while the Sunni look to tradition and law.

There are 22 Ahmaddiyya [1.3%] mosques. The Ahmaddiyya are a strongly missionary sect whose belief that their founder was the expected Messiah the majority of Muslims considers heretical. Its current world headquarters is in London.

This brief description of mosque affiliation is not comprehensive but it is enough to convey an impression of diversity. The situation could be further complicated by reference to a host of movements and groups that are active among UK Muslims. The dramatic growth of Islamism is probably the most significant movement among Muslims in Britain since the 1980s.[15]

Many non-Islamist Muslims believe that Islamists now dominate the public face of Islam in the UK. They would include the

---

14  Hamas in Gaza also originated from the Muslim Brotherhood.

15  For an excellent introdution to the world of Islamists by an insider who became a moderate Muslim see Ed Husain, *The Islamist: Why I joined radical Islam in Britain, What I saw Inside and why I left*, London: Penguin Books, 2007. See also Ian G. Williams, *Fundamentalist Movements within British Islam*, in Christopher H. Partridge, ed., *Fundamentalism*, Carlisle: Paternoster, 2001, pp. 75-92.

Muslim Council of Britain and the Islamic Foundation as Islamist bodies. But there are many shades of Islamism. Fundamental to any Islamist is the belief that the state should be subject to Muslim faith and practice. A British Islamist looks towards the goal when the British state will exist to uphold Muslim law. They differ on how that can be achieved and on the law that would be enforced in a Muslim British state.

Some believe that the only way to establish an Islamist state is by violent *jihad* [effort/struggle] while others believe that it can be established through a democratic process. Some long for the day when British society will be something like Saudi Arabia with everyone wearing Arabian clothes and the penal code including punishments such as stoning for adultery, limb amputation for theft and execution for apostasy from Islam. Others believe that a European Islamist state can accommodate to Western culture and that the Saudi type of penal code is amenable to reformation. Given this spectrum of views it is not surprising that some Islamists become terrorists while others condemn terrorism – but their common goal is a British Muslim-dominated state.

To complete the picture it has to be said that there are also 'ecumenical' aspects to the religions. Many Muslims will say that all types of Muslims are welcome to pray in their mosques and there are Hindu and Buddhist centres that claim to represent their religion as a whole. There are also organisations such as the Muslim Council of Britain or the Hindu Council UK that have been set up to represent the religions, especially to government. However, none of these bodies can truly represent the variety of adherents to their religion.

# Multiculturalism

As a concluding note for this chapter, in 1980 fostering cultural pluralism was government policy. This approach had been established in 1966 when Roy Jenkins was the Labour home secretary. He described what was then a new approach as 'integration'. This meant rejecting "a flattening process of assimilation" in favour of "equal opportunity, coupled with cultural diversity, in an atmosphere of mutual tolerance".[16] This policy meant that immigrants were encouraged to remain in the culture of the land of their origin – that it was good for Gujarati Hindus to live as Gujarati Hindus or Sri Lankan Buddhists as Sri Lankan Buddhists or Pakistani Muslims as Pakistani Muslims. This policy was unquestionably good in many ways not least as an antidote to the widespread racist response to immigrants. But 9/11 and particularly 7/7 in the UK has caused many to wonder whether untrammelled multiculturalism is the best policy.

---

16  Jenkins quoted in S.Poulter, *Ethnicity, Law and Human Rights*, Oxford Univ. Press, 1998, p.15-18.

# CHAPTER 2

# The evangelistic imperative

## Introduction

Evangelicals are 'good news' people. Standing firmly in the orthodox, Trinitarian, Reformation traditions we believe that we have
good news for everyone including adherents of the religions.
The good news is that God loved human beings so much that
the Father gave His only begotten Son, Jesus, up to death on a
cross so that whoever that is made alive by the Spirit so that they
believe in him will not perish but have eternal life. The greatest
responsibility and challenge facing evangelicals is to share this
good news with everyone. This is the evangelistic imperative.

Historically evangelicals have differed on a host of issues. They
even failed to establish a comprehensive international Evangelical Alliance in 1846 because of disagreement on the issue
of slavery. Even so, they did reach a consensus on the gospel
message of salvation and that consensus has prevailed to the
present in the Alliance's Basis of Faith. [1]

---

1   An international Evangelical Alliance was formed and many national
    alliances were inspired by the 1846 conference. For the story of the
    significant work of this movement see I. Randall and D. Hilborn, *One Body
    in Christ: The History and Significance of the Evangelical Alliance*, Carlisle:
    Paternoster, 2002.

In its description of salvation the Basis of Faith focuses on our human predicament, God's provision and the way we participate in God's provision.

# 1. Our human predicament

*The dignity of all people, made male and female in God's image to love, be holy and care for creation, yet corrupted by sin, which incurs divine wrath and judgment.*

# 2. God's provision

*The incarnation of God's eternal Son, the Lord Jesus Christ—born of the virgin Mary; truly divine and truly human, yet without sin.*

*The atoning sacrifice of Christ on the cross: dying in our place, paying the price of sin and defeating evil, so reconciling us with God.*

*The bodily resurrection of Christ, the first fruits of our resurrection; his ascension to the Father, and his reign and mediation as the only Saviour of the world.*

# 3. The way we participate in God's provision

*The justification of sinners solely by the grace of God through faith in Christ. The ministry of God the Holy Spirit, who leads us to repentance, unites us with Christ through new birth, empowers our discipleship and enables our witness.*

For evangelicals doctrine is not just words on a page but truth born in us by the power of the Spirit. God the Father gave the Son to die for us and sends the Spirit to make the sacrifice efficacious in us. Salvation is not only an act of God on our behalf but something that we experience as the Holy Spirit works within us. For evangelicals sorrow for sin and a longing to change [repentance] is an experience; trusting in Jesus for forgiveness so that we are freed from condemnation [new birth] is an experience; finding strength to defeat temptation and share the love of God in Jesus [discipleship and witness] is an experience. This is the core ministry of the Holy Spirit. The Spirit unites us with Jesus so that we enter into a relationship with God as our Father, Saviour and Advocate.

Evangelicals pray for and expect to see evidence of the Holy Spirit working in people's lives as they share the good news of Jesus' atoning work. This is what we long to see in the lives of all our neighbours whatever they believe. This is our bottom line. In one sense whether our neighbour belongs to a specific religion or not is immaterial. Their predicament is the same as any other human being and God's provision for them and the way they participate in God's provision is the same. Atheists, humanists, animists, nominal Christians, Hindus, Muslims etc all come to God the Father, through Jesus in the power of the Spirit if we come at all.

However, in reaching out to our religious neighbours the love of God demands that we reach out to them where they are. This means that we should strive to understand what religions are in general and the specific beliefs and practices of our neighbour's religion.

## A biblical understanding of religions

As evangelicals we turn to the Bible for our understanding of religions as we do for our understanding of the gospel. [2]

---

2   As John Stott says: 'We evangelicals are Bible people. We believe that God has spoken fully and finally in his Son Jesus Christ and in the biblical witness to Christ. We believe the scripture is precisely the written speech of God and that because it is God's word it has supreme authority over the Church." [*Who do Evangelicals Think they Are?* p. 4].

In the Bible there are just three New Testament references where a word occurs that can be translated as 'religion' (*thrēskeia*, Acts 26:5; Colossians 2:18: James 1:26-27). In Acts and Colossians it is Judaism that is in focus with the rituals, devotion and general conduct of the Jews to the fore. James focuses on what ought to be seen in the lives of those that claim to be worshippers of God through Jesus – acts of mercy to the needy and separation from the world. However, while the Bible speaks little of religion it is full of religious terminology that is focused on worship – what we do by way of recognition of the divine springing from the attitude of the heart and expressed in rituals and conduct.

## Idolatry

Fundamentally, what the Bible does is provide God's people with a mirror in which we can see whether we have been infected by a spiritual disease that is endemic in human beings in rebellion against the one true God. This disease is idolatry. Having rejected the authority and goodness of their Creator human beings look to various aspects of the created order for images of the divine.

## Idolatrous images of the divine

Here are some of the idolatrous images of the divine that appear in the Bible:

1  The poles of the goddess Ashteroth and the bulls of the god Baal. These were fertility gods. Their worship reflects the human desire for fecundity/prosperity. They can be seen as divine embodiments of our need for children and a secure food supply. The worship of fertility gods was fundamental to the Canaanites that were displaced by the

Israelites. God warned His people again and again that they should resist being drawn into this type of idolatry with assurances that he could and would provide for them if they remained faithful to him and his law.

2 The worship of the divine in the form of animals and reptiles and heavenly bodies such as the sun, moon and stars. Ezekiel has a vision of the leaders of the remnant left in Jerusalem secretly worshipping images of animals and reptiles in the temple. In the same vision he sees 25 men publically prostrating themselves before the sun and showing their backsides to the holy of holies in the process (Ezekiel 8).

3 In biblical times there is evidence that the gods, whatever their images were, were closely identified with the land where they were venerated so that the gods of the nation that dwelt in the land became identified with that nation. What the king of Assyria's commander in chief shouted to the Jews on the walls of Jerusalem in the time of Hezekiah is a clear illustration of this: "Do not listen to Hezekiah, for he is misleading you when he says, 'The Lord will deliver us.' Has the god of any nation ever delivered his land from the hand of the king of Assyria? Where are the gods of Hamath and Arpad? Where are the gods of Sepharvaim, Hena and Ivvah? Have they rescued Samaria from my hand? Who of all the gods of these countries has been able to save his land from me? How then can the Lord deliver Jerusalem from my hand?" (Isaiah 36:18-20 cf. 2 Kings 18:32-35). Here the military might of the nation has become the image of God.

## Idolatry as a mirror in which God's people can examine themselves

On the basis of the Bible it would be very easy for us as Christians to proclaim all religions other than Christianity as idolatrous. That is the truth. But if we would be content with this as the sum of what the Bible says about religion we would be profoundly mistaken. To do so would be to miss the fact that the overwhelming bulk of what is said about idolatry in the Bible is aimed at God's own people. The Bible's deep concern is the propensity of those that have experienced the goodness of God, often by means of startling divine interventions on their behalf, to forsake God and worship and serve idols.

The Bible is also clear that human beings either worship the one true Creator God or gods that they have created out of their own imagination. Therefore, even in our society that claims to be secular and claims to need no God, people are still worshiping gods of their own making. At its roots our culture, our society, is profoundly idolatrous. So, the first thing we must do when thinking about reaching out to people who are adherents of the religions is to make sure that we are not infected by the prevailing idolatry of our society.

In fact the gods of the Old Testament seem to be very much alive in the UK today. Ashtoreth and Baal may not have physical shrines but devotion to material prosperity is as intense now as it ever was among the Canaanites. The belief that our fate is guided by astral powers is as popular as ever and the belief that justice can only be established by violence – the myth of redemptive violence – is our daily media staple.

The only way we can prove that we are not idolaters is by the way we live. This is not to deny the importance of a right understanding of who God is and what He has done for us in Jesus the Messiah but to emphasise the clear teaching of the Bible that our 'religion' – our acts of worship and the way we live – is the only proof of the God we claim to serve. As James says: "Those who consider themselves religious and yet do not keep a tight rein on their tongues deceive themselves, and their religion is worthless. Religion that God our Father accepts as pure and faultless is this: to look after orphans and widows in their distress and to keep oneself from being polluted by the world" (James 1:26-27).

Rejecting the idols of our society, being passionate about justice for the weak and disadvantaged and controlling our tongues is sure evidence that we belong to God, the Father of our glorious Lord Jesus Christ. This very challenging biblical emphasis should cause us to approach those that belong to the religions with humility. Humility is also the right perspective from which to assimilate the biblical assessment of idolatry.

## The biblical assessment of idolatry

The overwhelming emphasis in the Bible is to dismiss the gods and the idols that represent them as non-entities. They are just works of human hands that have no power at all. The gods are as inert and useless as the metals or timber from which their idols are made. Here is a typical example:

Psalm 115:4-8
4   But their idols are silver and gold,
    made by human hands.
5   They have mouths, but cannot speak,
    eyes, but cannot see.
6   They have ears, but cannot hear,
    noses, but cannot smell.

7  *They have hands, but cannot feel,*
   *feet, but cannot walk,*
   *nor can they utter a sound with their throats.*
8  *Those who make them will be like them,*
   *and so will all who trust in them.*[3]

Many scholars have dismissed the view expressed by the Psalmist and prophets as naïve and unjust. Pluralists, who believe that all religions are equally valid attempts to represent the ultimate reality, are particularly dismissive of the biblical emphasis. But the biblical authors understood that idolaters viewed gods as spiritual realities that were represented by the physical idols. What they taught was that the gods as spiritual beings were non-entities – they did not exist to effect the good change that their worshippers craved.

When the Abiezrites came to demand that Gideon be handed over to them to be executed for destroying the altar of Baal and cutting down an Asherah pole his father's response was: "Are you going to plead Baal's cause…If Baal really is a god he can defend himself when someone breaks down his altar".[4] The standard biblical assessment of idolatry is that there is nothing more to idolatry than the tangible idol. The gods the idols represent are non-entities - they don't exist to hear and come to the aid of the devotees who cry to them for help. To look to them for help is utterly futile.

This extremely negative Old Testament assessment of idolatry is also Paul's assessment when in 1 Corinthians he comes

---

3  Cf. Isaiah 44:4-19; Jeremiah 10:3-14

4  Judges 6:31; cf. Elijah's taunting of the prophets of Baal on Mount Carmel in 1 Kings 18:27. Isaiah says that Bel and Nebo, as gods of Babylon, will be humiliated when their idols will be taken away into captivity (Is. 46:1).

to discuss food offered to idols: "So then, about eating food sacrificed to idols: We know that 'An idol is nothing at all in the world' and that 'There is no God but one.' For even if there are so-called gods, whether in heaven or on earth (as indeed there are many "gods" and many "lords"), yet for us there is but one God, the Father, from whom all things came and for whom we live; and there is but one Lord, Jesus Christ, through whom all things came and through whom we live" (1 Corinthians 8:4-6).

## Idolatry and the demonic

However, this pervasive biblical view is not the whole story because there are passages in the Old Testament that link idolatry with the demonic and Paul also draws on these passages in 1 Corinthians. There are just two Old Testament passages that say that idols are demonic – Deuteronomy 32:17 and Psalm 106:37.

The context of both passages is the unfaithfulness of Israel to Yahweh. In Deuteronomy Moses prophetically expresses God's disappointment that His people when they came to enjoy the prosperity that He had promised forsook Him and turned to worshipping other gods that are described by different terms – 'strange gods', 'abominations', 'demons', 'new gods' [NIV]. The word translated 'demons' refers to a well-known type of Mesopotamian spirit/demon. They were a bit like guardian angels but could damage as well as benefit the individuals in whom they had an interest. Therefore, it was important to keep them happy with offerings. Interestingly, no images were made of these spirits. A large proportion of religion worldwide has to do with this type of familiar/familial spirits. Belief in such beings is found among many adherents of the religions.

Psalm 106 is a long litany of Israel's unfaithfulness to the God who saved them. In verses 34-37 the psalmist focuses on their unfaithfulness in worshipping the idols of the land of Canaan that they had been commanded to destroy. The most heinous aspect of Canaanite worship that they adopted was the practice of sacrificing children. It is in this context that the psalm says "they sacrificed their sons and their daughters to demons". When idolatry leads to the appalling practice of child sacrifice it is clearly demonic.

So, although generally speaking idols are nothing – they are not real beings that can respond in blessing to their devotees - there are times when what they represent and what they demand open the door for the demonic to impact their devotees' lives. Ancient idolatry like contemporary idolatry is commonly accompanied by an active belief in many spirits – ancestral spirits or spirit beings that have a direct impact on human life, that can be manipulated and that need appeasing. This is the aspect of historical religion that is the context for the demonic possession/oppression that is confronted by Jesus and that is always a reality in the life of the church.

Having declared in 1 Corinthians 8:4 that an idol is nothing, in 1 Corinthians 10:20 Paul also says that "the sacrifices of pagans are offered to demons, not to God, and I do not want you to be participants with demons". The explanation for the different approach taken by Paul in the two passages is the approximation to idolatrous acts. In the first case Paul has in view buying meat in the market that may have been offered to a god. In that case a Christian is free to buy and eat without any anxiety because an idol is nothing – although even in this case restraint should be exercised if buying and eating would offend a weaker Christian. In the second case what is in view is participating in an idolatrous ritual meal in the temple. This is participation at a wholly different level and could lead to the believer seeming to give approval to practices that are clearly demonic in that they would be completely contrary to God's will. Temple prostitution would be a good example of such demonic practices. Paul is not focusing here on evil spirits that can possess and oppress people but on involvement with idolatrous ritual that has evil moral consequences. The background is Psalm 106 rather than Deuteronomy 32.

## Idolatry and the truth about God

Since the Bible is very negative about idolatry does that mean that we as evangelicals must be very negative towards the religions because their gods are idols? Does that mean that all we can do is shun them and take every opportunity to expose them as false? We should certainly be distressed by idol worship and especially by the idol worship that dominates our Western culture as Paul was "greatly distressed to see that the city [of Athens] was full of idols" (Acts 17:16). But the Athenian devotion to idols did not mean that they were totally ignorant of the true God.

Paul certainly believed that this was the case as he shared the good news of Jesus with them. The section of the address that is particularly relevant in this context is where Paul argues that it was God's intention that human beings should be divided into nations with their unique geographical locations and histories. God's purpose for these 'cultural factories' was to create a conducive context for people to seek him "and perhaps reach out for him and find him, though he is not far from any of us". Paul then quotes a couple of Greek philosophers/poets who clearly had an inkling of this truth that God is close/immanent to us: "For in him we live and move and have our being." As some of your own poets have said, 'We are his offspring'" (Acts

17:26-28). The first quote was from the Cretan Epimenides and the second from the Cilician Aratus. Epimenides and Aratus may well have been idolaters but they had said things about God that is true. By taking hold of their glimpses of the true God Paul hoped to draw his Athenian listeners into the full revelation that he had to share with them.

## Common grace and general revelation

In Christian theology the fact that there are practices and beliefs in every religious tradition that are reminiscent of the truth has traditionally been attributed to 'common grace' and 'general revelation'.

Common grace has to do with God's continuing goodness towards His creation despite human rebellion and its consequences for the rest of creation. After the flood, God covenanted to sustain the creation so that it remained a sustainable context for human life despite our sin. Not only does God ensure that the earth continues to produce what we need to sustain us but that the formation of government and other aspects of culture, such as the arts, that enhance the quality of our life, are also possible. This flourishing of culture is deeply impacted by our sin but that it happens at all is a witness to God's common grace – his unmerited favour to us despite our rebellion against him. It would be amazing, therefore, if we were not able to find hints of God's goodness in any culture that makes it possible for us to talk intelligibly about Him.

As we reach out to adherents of non-Christian religions it is helpful to get to know not only their religious ideas and practices but also their culture in general. Because of God's common grace we are sure to discover something in their culture that will help us to make the message of the gospel more intelligible.

General revelation is the theological idea that who God is can be deduced from observing creation/the natural world. The idea is based on scriptures such as Psalm 19, ("The heavens declare the glory of God..."), and Romans 1:18-20. In Romans, Paul argues that who God is – "His eternal power and divine nature – have been clearly seen, being understood from what has been made" (Romans 1:20). The problem is that as rebellious human beings we refuse to acknowledge this obvious truth. Paul uses very strong language at this point and writes of the "wickedness of human beings who suppress the truth by their wickedness" (Romans 1:18). As human beings we reject the reality of God that stares us in the face as we observe His creation because His reality demands that we surrender our autonomy. But because we have been made for worship we cannot live without some god/s. So, as Paul argues, human beings create their own gods – "they exchanged the glory of the immortal God for images made to look like mortal human beings and birds and animals and reptiles" (Romans 1:23).

What Paul says about God's general revelation in Romans 1 lays bare the root cause of idolatry in the human heart. In this context the 'original' sin is to suppress the truth that God is our Creator and Lord so that we are free to create gods that are less awesome and holy. Idolatry is the result of failing to recognise God's glory in His creation and leads to Paul's conclusion in Romans 3:23 that "all have sinned and fall short of the glory of God".[5] Having established this truth the rest of Romans has to do with how God through Jesus the Messiah and in the power of the Spirit has dealt with the root cause of idolatry in the human heart.

---

5   By Romans 3 Paul has also argued that Israel, despite having received God's special revelation, must also be included among those that have sinned and fall short of God's glory.

Through faith in Jesus we are indwelt by the Spirit and are not under the control of the sinful nature. We do not suppress the truth about God but embrace it and glory in it. However, until we die or until the Lord returns our renewed heart/spirit will have to contend with our defeated sinful nature and its tendency to idolatry. So, the tendency of Israel in the OT to turn their back on the truth of God and worship idols remains as a very salutary lesson to us as disciples of Jesus. The experience of Israel is primarily meant for us as Christians. When we are wont to condemn the idolatry of adherents of other religions we should be careful to make sure that we are free from idolatry ourselves because the tendency to idolatry is still very real within us. Better, maybe, to listen to the command of our Lord Jesus: "Do not judge, or you too will be judged" (Matthew 7:1).

The biblical contention that as human beings we know the truth about God in our hearts but choose to suppress that knowledge means that we are essentially religious beings. Since we are created in God's image we must worship and if we don't worship the true God then we will find something or someone else to worship. This means that we have a religious consciousness that has to find expression in some form or another.

J. H. Bavinck is one of the few evangelical missiologists who have tried to describe the religious consciousness of human beings that suppress the general revelation of God in creation. According to Bavinck our human existence as worshipping beings forces us to face certain issues and the questions they engender. He calls these "magnetic points" in our religious consciousness and lists five of them:

1 *I and the cosmos*. Human beings sense that they belong to the created order. In a very real sense we feel that we are a part of nature/the cosmos. The question that arises from this feeling is, what exactly is our relationship to the cosmos?

2 *I and the norm*. Bavinck calls this the "religious norm". There is something in us that tells us that we should not do exactly what we want – that there must be rules for us to follow.

3 *I and the riddle of my existence*. On the one hand we believe that we can achieve something – we can plan, build and change our future by our actions. But on the other hand circumstances are often beyond our power to control – so that whatever we do can be over-run by what we call fate or destiny. We are left puzzling between the conflicting forces of freedom and determinism.

4 *I and salvation*. History and contemporary experience testify to the fact that we are very conscious as human beings that things are not as they should be. There are things that are wrong with nature itself and with the way in which we are too. But faced with this we long for things to be different – we long for salvation.

5 *I and the Supreme Power*. Human beings have never been content with the visible but have sought a reality beyond what can be seen. What is more we believe that the meaning of our human life can only be found in relation to that which lies beyond it.[6]

----

6    J. H. Bavinck, *The Church Between the Temple and Mosque, A Study of the Relationship Between the Christian Faith and other Religions*, Grand Rapids, Eerdmans, 1961, pp. 32-33

In light of common grace and general revelation these five magnetic points described by Bavinck provide a whole wealth of sources for us to reach out with the gospel. Every religion is a response to these riddles and has answers to the questions that provide many points at which we can begin to explain the true answers found in the revelation of God in Jesus.

A popular way of expressing the relationship between the answers in the religions to the questions generated by the riddles of our human existence and the answers found in the revelation in Jesus Christ is that the latter fulfils the former. Two examples from very different periods in church history will illustrate the nature – and risks – of this approach.

Justin Martyr (c. 100-165 AD) was a missionary, who as his name implies, paid for his life for his witness to Jesus. He came to faith after a long pilgrimage through some of the major philosophical schools of his day. Originating in Palestine he ended up teaching as a Christian philosopher in Rome. Some of his work as an apologist for the Christian faith in an increasingly hostile Roman context has survived.

In assessing his thought it is important to remember that he was writing as an apologist trying to persuade the Roman authorities that the Christian faith was not totally alien to the Greco-Roman religious-philosophical tradition. What we find in his apologies, therefore, does not give us a full view of his orthodox Christian faith.

He based his defence of the Christian faith on the description of Jesus Christ as the word [logos] of God in John 1:1-5. It was through the idea of the logos, which is important in Greek philosophy, that Justin was able to argue that the heart of the Christian faith was not totally alien but a fulfilment of that tradition. Using the Stoic concept of 'seeds of the logos' [*logos spermatikos*] he argued that the pre-existent Christ had been at work in the minds of the philosophers so that they had correctly deduced Christian truths such as the creation, the Trinity and final judgment. So, just as the Old Testament was a preparation for the coming of the Christ for the Jews, Greek philosophy was a preparation for the Gentiles. [7] However, Justin also believed that on the cross Jesus had defeated the devil so that people could be freed from his power by faith in Jesus. This way of salvation meant rejecting Roman idolatry and it was this rejection that cost Justin his life.

Justin's thought has been used by contemporary scholars[8] to justify the position that all religions are a preparation for the gospel and that Jesus has fulfilled all religions (inclusivism). The fact that the guardians of Roman religion were not convinced by his argument and put him to death shows that religious people may not always find the inclusivist argument convincing – with very unpleasant consequences for those that espouse it. If we do argue that Jesus Christ fulfils the longings of the religions we must expect their adherents to believe that our argument is subversive. In the last analysis there is no way to avoid the offence of the cross to the proud human heart. Justin may have gone too far in trying to make the gospel intelligible to his educated Roman contemporaries but that should not

---

7    Justin also believed that Plato had been directly influenced by Moses. This claim is still unproven but reminds us that the religions did not develop in total isolation from each other. For a full discussion of the reasons for reminscences of truth in the religions see Dan Strange, Their Rock is not our Rock, Grand Rapids, Zondervan, 2014, pp. 246-260.

8    Discussed in Alistair McGrath, *Christian Theology: An Introduction 6th Edition,* Oxford: Wiley, 2016 p419

deter us from learning about our neighbours' religion in order to make the gospel more understandable to them.

The second example comes from the work of Don Richardson who was a Regions Beyond Missionary Union missionary among the Sawi people of Western New Guinea, Indonesia, from 1962-72. Richardson, with his wife and baby daughter, went to live among the Sawi that were known as cannibalistic headhunters. With much effort he became fluent in their very complex language but discovered that their religion and culture made it very hard for them to embrace the gospel. For example, in the account of the crucifixion they saw Judas as the hero and Jesus as the fool. Because of the incessant conflict between the village they lived in and other villages the Richardson family eventually decided that they had to leave. Wanting to keep them there the Sawi villages decided to make peace and it was the way in which they did this that provided the key for their acceptance of the gospel. They made peace by means of a peace child. A father would take one of his children and present it to the enemy villagers as a peace offering. They believed that if my enemy can trust me with one of his own children then he couldn't continue to be my enemy. Richardson saw this practice as a 'redemptive analogy' that enabled him to explain in a way that made sense to the Sawi that God had presented his own Son as a sacrifice so that he could make peace with people that were his enemies. Following this realisation many Sawi came to believe. Subsequently Richardson left Indonesia and eventually joined the US Center for World Mission where he launched the Perspective on the World Christian Movement course that advocates the importance of 'redemptive analogies' as a crucial means to communicate the gospel.

# Idolatry, religion and culture

The change that occurred in the relation between religion and culture in the climax of God's revelation in Jesus is very significant in this context. In the OT covenant God rescued a nation from slavery and gave them ritual and moral laws and land. By keeping the law in their land out of gratitude to their redeemer God they were a light to the nations – a revelation of God's purposes for humanity and the earth. There were times when God's purpose for Israel was partially fulfilled such as during the reigns of Solomon and David. But overall God's intention was thwarted by the people's tendency to conform to the idolatry of their neighbours. This was no surprise to God but Israel's incorrigibility underlined the need expressed by the prophets for a covenant that would effect change at the deepest level of human existence – the heart.

In the new covenant Jesus Christ (the Messiah) fulfilled all aspects of the old covenant and in doing so took over the role that Israel had of being a blessing to the nations. The nation with its land and temple in Jerusalem found its fulfilment in the person of God's incarnate Son who suffered and died on the cross for the sins of the world and who rose again victorious over death and was exalted to God's right hand. As a result access to God became available to anyone through faith in Jesus. Belonging to God no longer meant belonging to a specific nation linked to a specific bit of earth and observing particular rituals focused on the sanctuary in Jerusalem. This meant that the most fundamental question that the followers of Jesus faced at the beginning was whether a disciple had to be a Jew to be an authentic member of the community of Jesus.

At the Council of Jerusalem (Acts 15) the leaders of the Christian community that was by then growing rapidly among non-Jews decided that it was not necessary to be a Jew to be a disciple of Jesus. In summing up the discussion at the Council of Jerusalem James said that out of respect for the Jews that were scattered throughout the Roman Empire the letter that was sent from the Council to the Christian communities that were already made up mainly of non-Jews/Gentiles asked them to avoid certain things – "food sacrificed to idols, from blood, from the meat of strangled animals and from sexual immorality" (Acts 15:29).

What is so radical about the Jerusalem Council decision is that what the Jews regarded as fundamental to membership of God's people is reduced to the level of culture. For the Jew circumcision, the dietary laws and the cult based in Jerusalem was essential to being included in God's covenant. This is what made them the people of God and, so, observing these require-ments was essential to belonging to God's people – to salvation. But in the new covenant these become cultural characteristics of Jewish identity. If to be Jews males had to be circumcised, food law had to be observed and rituals respected then such regulations could be respected. But in the Christian community of the new covenant in Jesus the Messiah the link between such regulations and salvation was decisively cut. In fact Paul argues that the observance of rules and regulations had never been the ground of salvation even in Israel – that it had always been a heart response in faith to the grace and mercy of God. What the coming of the Messiah did was to make this very explicit so that the door of salvation was open for everyone.

Although the Jews have a unique relationship to the gospel of Jesus the Messiah their experience is very relevant to the adher-ents of other religions. As with Judaism religion is always deeply entwined with culture. The decision of the Jerusalem Council shows that it is possible to distinguish between what is cultural and what belongs to the essence of the gospel. Jewish Christians in New Testament times continued to observe many practices that identified them as Jews and that had been observed for centuries. Circumcision, the dietary laws and the temple cult have already been mentioned. Another was the taking of vows and the temple ritual associated with their observance. Paul saw no reason why he as the apostle of the Gentiles should not accede to a request by the leaders of the Church in Jerusalem to take a vow and, with four other Jewish Christians, go through the temple rituals associated with it (Acts 21:23-24).

This distinction between the core of the Christian faith rooted in Judaism and the cultural traditions associated with it has been at the heart of missiological thinking in the last half century. A good example is the discussion – sometimes heated - among evangelical missiologists focused on 'insider movements'.[9] These are movements of people who say that they are disciples of Jesus but who continue to live within their traditional religious culture. Understandably Western evangelical missiologists have been very concerned about the point at which these 'insider' believers become genuine fully-fledged evangelical Christians.

Many issues in this often-heated discussion are unresolved but it has made one thing very clear: there are many aspects of any religion, including our own, that do not belong to the essence of a religion but are cultural accretions. Our greatest

---

9  For a good introduction to the insider movement and the debate it has generated see http://www.lausanne.org/content/muslim-followers-of-jesus

need is discernment to see what is cultural and what is essential and the best way to discernment is to focus on the essential in our witness. There will be times when we will be unconcerned about those that claim to be disciples of Jesus continuing to observe certain traditional cultural practices. An example could be the use of prayer beads by Muslim disciples of Jesus to remind them of the names of God. But there will be times when the incompatibility of observing a traditional practice with being a disciple of Jesus will have to be insisted upon.

The conflict between Paul and Peter in Antioch over the Jewish dietary law is an excellent example of the gospel essential trumping traditional religious culture. Peter had been taught through his vision in Joppa and his subsequent experience in the house of Cornelius that the dietary laws were no longer valid as a marker of belonging to the people of God. On hearing the message of the gospel a Gentile and his household had believed and been baptised in the Spirit. Paul, the fanatical traditionalist, had likewise by direct revelation encountered the risen Lord. He too was baptised in the Spirit (Acts 9:17) and commissioned to preach the gospel to the Gentiles. Paul also understood that the gospel broke down all barriers between people and especially the biggest barrier of all being the barrier between God's OT people and everyone else (Ephesians 2:11-22).

So, if a Gentile believer is accepted into God's kingdom on exactly the same terms as a Jew and both enjoy the blessings of the kingdom – especially the indwelling Holy Spirit – in exactly the same way then nothing should be allowed to hinder their friendship and fellowship. Since a meal became central to the life of the church from the beginning the issue of the continuing validity or not of the Jewish dietary law had to be faced.

With the exile and scattering of the Jews among the nations in the sixth century BC dietary law had become very significant to the Jews as a marker of their identity and a hindrance to their assimilation with the people among whom they lived – including assimilation into their idolatrous ways. That the dietary laws made it almost impossible for Jews to eat with Gentiles/non-Jews was considered vital to the preservation of their faith and identity. It is not surprising, therefore, that some Jewish Christians found it very difficult to let go of this law. When some of them heard that Jewish Christians in Syrian Antioch were eating with Gentile Christians they travelled there to persuade the Jewish Christians to desist and continue to observe the dietary law. Peter, Barnabas and Paul were in Antioch at that time and Paul gives us an account of what happened in Galatians 2:11-14.

Peter, and even Barnabas, were persuaded by these Jewish Christians to stop eating with Gentile Christians. Paul says that he openly opposed Peter when he did this because his conduct was not "in line with the truth of the gospel" (Galatians 2:12). In light of the gospel the dietary law had become a cultural tradition that hindered the outworking of the life of the Spirit among God's New Testament people and to continue to observe it was to resist God's purpose. That Christians were one in Christ had to find expression in sharing food together. If traditional cultural practice made this impossible then it had to be laid aside for the sake of the gospel.

The way in which the early Church dealt with the Jewish cultural/religious legacy in light of the gospel provides a pattern for Christian mission to adherents of the religions. The history of mission testifies that there have been aspects of all cultures that are both compatible and incompatible with the gospel.

Therefore, as we reach out to adherents of the religions in the UK we need to keep in mind that:

1 The core of a religion can be distinguished from the traditional cultural accretions that have come to be entwined with it. This is true of all religions including Christianity.

2 The continuing validity and value of any traditional cultural practice is determined in light of the truth of the gospel.

3 The gospel will affirm some traditional cultural practices and reject others.

## Contextualisation

The process of adapting the gospel to a non-Christian religion and culture has come to be known as contextualisation. The term was first used in World Council of Churches circles in the 1970s but was quickly adopted and redefined by evangelicals. It has been the subject of much controversy but the following definition by Scott Moreau is now generally accepted as a valid approach in evangelical mission:

> "...contextualization can be described as 'the process whereby Christians adapt the forms, content, and praxis of the Christian faith so as to communicate it to the minds and hearts of people with other cultural backgrounds. The goal is to make the Christian faith as a whole - not only the message but also the means of living out of our faith in the local setting - understandable.'" [10]

---

10  A. Scott Moreau, *Contextialisation in World Missions: Mapping and Assessing Evangelical Models*, Kregel Academic, 2012, p. 36

Just one story from the Buddhist/Shinto/Confucian/folk religion context of Japan will suffice to justify the need to adapt the gospel message to the cultural context in which it is being shared:

> "A missionary was preaching the gospel in a public evangelistic meeting [in Japan]. Toward the end of his talk he gave the usual impassioned plea: 'If you accept Jesus Christ as your personal Lord and Saviour, you will have everlasting life. This means that after you die on earth, you will go to heaven where you will live forever.' ... After the meeting, however, an elderly lady came up and expressed her concerns to the missionary. 'Teacher, why do you assume that we want to live forever? Besides, I don't want to go to heaven. When I die, I want to be where my ancestors are.'" [11]

For Buddhists, eternal life is the problem. They believe that human beings are trapped in an endless cycle of reincarnation into lives that are dominated by suffering. They hope for the end of 'life' not its eternal continuation. And for traditionally devout Japanese people ancestors play a crucial role in their family and communal life as is witnessed by their central place in at least three annual festivals. It is these living ancestors that exist to bless their families and communities that the elderly Japanese lady wanted to join when she died.

It is beyond the scope of this resource to explore the theological and missiological ramifications of this one example in detail but some obvious observations can be made:

---

11  R. Dowsett ed., *Global Mission: Reflections and Case Studies in Contextualization for the Whole Church*, William Carey library, Pasadena, 2011, p. 97

1 Attempting to adapt the gospel message to a particular religious/cultural context cannot mean denying the crucial role of the Holy Spirit in opening our darkened minds to the truth of the gospel.

2 Seeking to make the gospel as intelligible as possible within any culture is an act of love. It is out of compassion that we want to remove as many barriers as we can that hinder people from hearing the good news of Jesus the Messiah.

3 Any attempt to adapt the message must be firmly rooted in biblical truth. Evangelical contextualisation does not mean accepting that the beliefs and practices of those we are attempting to reach have an equal validity with biblical truth. But it does mean that we subject our own understanding of biblical truth as well as the beliefs and practices of those we are trying to reach to the authority of the Bible.

4 As we seek to understand adherents of non-Christian religion and look for biblical resources to share the gospel message in a way that will be more intelligible to them we will find that our appreciation of the gospel will be deepened.

5 Taking seriously how someone from another religion will hear our presentation of the good news of Jesus highlights the way in which our presentation has been shaped by our own culture. In the case of the elderly Japanese lady the heavy emphasis on the individual's faith in Jesus so that the individual can enjoy eternal life reflects our Western individualist culture that became dominant in the 18th century.[12]

6 When we turn to the Bible in light of the sort of challenge posed by the elderly Japanese lady more often than not we

---

12 For a brief and helpful discussion of 'Individualism' see *Faith and Nation: Report of a Commission of Inquiry to the UK Evangelical Alliance,* pp. 32-24. Available at http://eauk.org/current-affairs/publications/faith-and-nation.cfm

will see that our presentation of the good news is clearly inadequate. In her case God's purpose in Christ is not just the salvation of individuals – however glorious that is – but the renewal of humanity and the rest of creation. This is not the place for a full discussion but the fact that the New Testament images/pictures of salvation are overwhelmingly corporate/communal is very relevant here.

7  We should not be afraid to contextualise the gospel because up to now Christian missionaries have not found any culture that is totally impervious to their message. One of the glories of our message is that it is translatable into every culture. The work of Bible translation is often very challenging but no language – which is the bearer of culture – has yet been found into which it is impossible to translate the Bible.

## Conclusion

In the 18th century William Carey[13] demolished the Reformed argument that the great commission given by Jesus to his followers to "go and make disciples of all nations" (Matthew 28:19) had been fulfilled and was no longer binding. This led to an explosion of evangelical missionary work from the UK to every corner of the earth. This movement took the command to make disciples of all nations very seriously with its insistence that people of all nations needed to hear the good news of the kingdom in their own language and that the scriptures should be translated into their language as soon as was practically possible. This meant that all evangelical missionaries had to listen as well as speak to fulfil their mission.

---

13  Carey, William *An Enquiry into the Obligations of Christians to Use Means for the Conversion of the Heathen* (1792)

In the second half of the 20th century many thousands came to live in the UK from the nations to which we traditionally sent missionaries. They have come with their languages, traditions and religions. Since the 1960s it has even been government policy to encourage them to hang on to their national identity.[14] In consequence in the UK we no longer have to go very far to attempt to make disciples from other nations because the nations have come to us. But do the principles of the evangelical missionary movement still apply? Must we strive to relate to them in their languages so that we can share the gospel in what may very well still be their heart language even after many years of living in the UK?

Amazingly the second most common mother tongue after English in the UK is now Mirpuri Pahari. This is the language of well over 60 per cent of people of Pakistani origin.[15] It is a language with a minimal printed literature and some non-print material such as songs, stories and Islamic instruction. A small beginning has been made in translating the Bible and some non-print Christian material is also available. But what is available seems very little to serve more than 500,000 people. [16]

The need to listen and understand our religious neighbours so that we can share the gospel with them is as necessary as ever. We listen in order to be able to share the gospel in a way

-------

14 The wisdom or not of this policy will be discussed in Chapter 7

15 For a study of the use and significance of Mirpuri Pahari see M. And L. Lothers, *Mirpuri Immigrants in England: A sociolinguistic Survey*, SIL International, 2012

16 For the non-print material published by Word of Life see http://www.word-of-life.org/category-s/101.htm

that will be more intelligible to someone from another religion and culture. As we saw in the case of Justin Martyr this process can lead to the conclusion that the adherents of another religion have already come a long way in the direction of the truth. Others are more skeptical and see what Richardson calls "redemptive analogies" as merely convenient cultural hooks on which to hang the gospel message. There is probably a range of views between these two poles among evangelicals today. But all are agreed that Jesus the Messiah is the redemptive reality that is hinted at in the analogy and the Truth that was perceived in the truths.

To say that Jesus fulfils the redemptive analogies in a religion or culture is not the same as saying that a Christian culture is superior to a Hindu, Buddhist, Sikh, Muslim, etc culture. We don't listen in order to be able to win a battle in a war of cultures. One of the most valuable lessons of contextualisation has been to make missionaries conscious of the cultural baggage that we carry with the precious message of the gospel. Even in a country that has been heavily influenced by the gospel it is possible for traditions to develop that are not essential to it, can be inconsistent with it and even contradictory to it. This is not a call to be negative about our own culture but to be realistic and honest – and prepared to bring even our own culture, including our Christian traditions, under the authority of the Bible. To do so is bound to destroy any temptation to triumphalism.

Another great benefit of being conscious of our own cultural baggage is the realisation that we are not involved in a battle against idolatry as those that are free of the danger of idolatry. This does not mean that we diminish the seriousness of worshipping anything or anyone other than the God that has revealed himself fully to humankind in Jesus Christ. The Bible is absolutely clear on the vanity and wickedness that is so often associated with idolatry. But the Bible is equally clear on the great danger of God's people falling into idolatry. Idolatry is the default religion of fallen human beings. It is the multi-form religion of our common sinful nature. When we trust in Jesus as Lord we are freed from the inevitability but not from the threat of idolatry. Our only security is to continually cultivate our relationship with God through Jesus in the power of the Holy Spirit so that we can live in/by the Spirit. As we reach out with the gospel to adherents of other religions we must keep in mind that our own culture, however much it has been formed by Christianity in the past, can be idolatrous.

CHAPTER 3

# Evangelising people of other religions: recent evangelical approaches

*"There is no fear in love. But perfect love drives out fear"*
1 John 4:18.

## At the heart is love

What we need, above all, is love. As people of the religions increasingly populate parts of our cities and their religious buildings replace church buildings, it is understandable that the people that remain from another age and culture are discomforted or even fearful. Fellow evangelicals may tell us about the aim of Muslim mission to take over Britain and establish a state run according to *shari'a*. When this is coupled with knowledge of the significant growth of Islam and the constant attention to radical Islam in the media, it is not surprising that some evangelicals are tempted to be afraid.

In response some are attracted to the historic Christendom model of the relationship between the Church and state and call for the protection and privileging of the Church by law as a defence against the domination by any other religion. This involves legally defining the UK as a Christian state and affirms the conviction of adherents of other religions that when British power is aimed at their co-religionists that it is Christianity that is fighting against them.

But a desire to defend ourselves by means of the power of the state falls short of the kingdom rule of Jesus our Messiah.[1] He commands us to love even our enemies (Matthew 5:44), to "do to others what you would have them do to you" (Matthew 7:12), and to love God with everything that we are and have and our neighbour as ourselves (Matthew 22:37-38; Mark 12:29-31). And we "know what love is" because "Jesus Christ laid down his life for us" (1 John 3:16). What Ida Glaser says about love of Muslims can be applied to all the religions:

> *"As Jesus' focus was on saving others rather than on saving himself… so our focus needs to be on the eternal welfare of Muslim people rather than on showing Christian superiority or limiting Islamic rule. This makes evangelism and all that goes with it a priority, but it also determines how we relate to Muslims at every level. In particular… it is important that the cross is the way Jesus faces the worst of the fallen human world. It should therefore guide our response to what we might see as the worst as well as the best aspects of the world of Islam; and it should remind us how much potential there is for sin in us as we relate to Muslims."[2]*

1   For a very interesting argument that the 'Casting your perls before swine' saying in Matthew 7:6 is referring to entrusting the propagation of the good news of the gospel to the power of the state see G.H.Stassen and D.P.Gushee, *Kingdom Ethics*, Downers Grove, IVP, 2003, p. 457ff

2   Ida Glaser, "Thinking Biblically About Islam" in S.Bell and C.Chapman [eds], *Between Naivety and Hostility: Uncovering the best Christian responses to Islam in Britain*, Milton Keynes, Authentic, 2011, pp. 24-5.

It was love that led God's Son to become incarnate. "The Word became flesh and made his dwelling among us" (John 1:14). Evangelicals have been conscious of the need to reach out with the gospel into communities facing social and economic deprivation, especially in the inner cities, that have been abandoned by most of the churches. There are some churches and a number of agencies, such as City Missions, Fresh Expressions and Urban Expression, that focus on this need. These churches and agencies focus on incarnational love – they emphasise that the only way to reach a community is to live in it, belong to it and serve it. Some of these intentional missional communities may well be working in areas dominated by adherents of the religions but there is no evidence of a widespread movement among evangelicals to reach out in this way.

If reaching our Muslim, Hindu or Sikh friends with the gospel is a priority then some of us must go and live where they are and we will need agencies to help people do this as we help people do it in many countries abroad. The Mahabba[3] Network is a substantial step in the right direction. The idea for the network was born in response to the 9/11 and 7/7 atrocities. The vision is to encourage Christians who want to respond in love to our Muslim neighbours to meet together to pray and to reach out with the gospel. The groups that now meet in many cities come from various denominations and churches. They are helped by specialists to reach out to Muslims and to be catalysts for reaching out in their churches. The network is also working on various resources to help Muslims that become disciples of Jesus to integrate into existing churches or to live as disciples in their own communities.

---

3    'Mahabba' means 'love' in Arabic

The need for Christians to be where adherents of the religions are is a matter of urgency. Many of those involved with reaching out are convinced that at the heart of any effective church or ministry to them is a loving, accepting, welcoming community of God's people. This is the essential base for witness and growth as disciples. This love may be expressed through:

- Unconditional acceptance of people of any background and stage of understanding about following Jesus.
- Serving each other and the wider community, meeting practical needs and doing things together.
- Allowing space for different groups to meet and express their faith and devotion in different styles and languages.
- Learning to accept different styles of leadership, meetings and cultural practices, as we live and work together.
- Seeing how God's word applies in our different cultures, so that we can help each other to obey it.

We owe everything to God's unconditional love, forgiveness and grace, shown to us in Jesus. We need to reflect that grace to each other.[4]

As Manoj Raithatha, of the South Asian Forum of the Evangelical Alliance said: "We need to get back to the early Church's emphasis on relationships, hospitality and family" (BBC Radio 4 *Sunday* programme, 17 June, 2012).

## Understanding adherents of other religions

A meeting with a lecturer on Buddhism at the Sihanouk Reaj University in Phnom Penh, Cambodia, is one of the most

---

4   See *Engaging with Hindus,* pages 105-116 for specific suggestions for churches

memorable meetings that I had as Tearfund's theological advisor. The lecturer was a Sri Lankan Buddhist scholar whose attack on Christian missions in a public lecture, in which he described them as 'parasites', had been reported in the press. Having asked my colleague in Phnom Penh to arrange opportunities for me to get an understanding of Cambodian Buddhism he managed to arrange a meeting with this very anti-Christian lecturer. It was not surprising that the atmosphere was somewhat frosty at the beginning of our meeting. I began by asking him to tell me why he was so antagonistic to Christian missions. His main objection was his perception that Christian missions used aid and development as bait to lure people away from their traditional culture – that includes their Buddhist religion – into a Western culture – that includes Christianity.

I didn't go to the meeting with a clear plan of action but with the naïve opinion that since the lecturer had strongly expressed his poor opinion of Christian mission in public, it would be a good starting point to find out why. The host of Western evangelical agencies with an emphasis on care of the poor that were flooding into Cambodia at that time was the occasion for his outburst. But his reaction was also informed by a deep prejudice formed by Sri Lanka's colonial history.

Most adherents of the religions have a high regard for Jesus. But with most of them sharing the colonial history of the Sri Lankan lecturer they may have very negative perceptions of Christianity:

- **Christianity is the same as Western culture**: For Asians generally, religion, culture and community are tightly linked. You are born into your community and therefore into your culture and religion. Christianity is regarded as a religion in which there is freedom, but probably too much freedom, which leads to permissiveness. Whatever most adherents of the religions see of Western culture in the media they assume to be typical of Christian culture. They want what is good in Western culture while retaining their own cultural identity.

- **The way to God**: Hindus, Sikhs and Buddhists see all religions as essentially the same – different ways to God. Muslims on the other hand believe that theirs is the only fully valid way to God. So they all believe that leaving your religion/ community is unnecessary and wrong. When people speak about 'becoming a Christian' or 'coming to church', what they hear is 'become Western' or 'join our community'.

- **For them the concept of conversion is a huge obstacle:** Conversion is a sensitive and controversial issue. Muslims accept the idea, but see only one direction as valid: leaving Islam is apostasy. For Hindus and Sikhs the concept is alien and unacceptable. The reasons, consistently in the 300 years since the beginnings of the Protestant missionary movement in India, include *the perceived threat to family, community and culture, the social and political implications, the links with the colonial past,* and above all *the sense of religious exclusiveness.* "Changing your religion is the greatest sin on earth. It is like changing your mother," said a listener to a Radio Leicester programme on conversion.[5]

---

5   For a full discussion of the issues of conversion in the Indian context, see Sebastian. Kim, *In Search of Identity: Debates on Religious Conversion in India.* New Delhi: Oxford University Press, 2003.
    See further the paper from NIFCON on Robin Thomson 'Evangelism, Conversion and Hindu relations' in *Relating with Hindu diaspora: Anglican and Lutheran reflections* Mosher, Wingate & Raja (Eds) pp53-55 http://nifcon.anglicancommunion.org/media/217611/

- **Christians in countries like India and Pakistan are poor people who were exploited by missionaries** - in the past and still in the present.
- **Some of them may have had bad experiences of racism.**
- **Many may be quite content to remain within their own community.** At the same time they may be experiencing considerable tension and looking for answers.

# Experiencing church meetings

Much has been said about the cultural gap between secular people and church practice. What we do when we gather together as church is probably even more alien to our non-Christian religious friends as it is to our secular friends. They will find the following very strange:

- Not taking shoes off when entering a holy building.
- Sitting on pews/chairs to worship – rather than on the floor.
- Western music, whether the traditional organ and choir or the modern band. For Muslims the whole idea of worshipping God in congregational song would be odd.
- The way in which a holy book is treated – for example, a Muslim would never put a copy of the Qur'an on the floor and a holy book should look like a holy book. A paperback copy of the Qur'an would be considered very disrespectful.
- Physical posture – in Muslim worship submission to God is expressed physically by prostration.

NIFCON-Booklet_Relating-with-Hindu-Diaspora.pdf
Ebe Sunder Raj, *National Debate on Conversion*. Chennai: Bharat Jyoti, 2001.
Robin Thomson, *Changing India: Insights from the Margin*. New Delhi: BR Publications, 2002.
Andrew Wingate, *The Church and Conversion*. New Delhi: ISPCK, 1997.
Robin Thomson, *Engaging with Hindus*, Good Book Company, 2014

**Ram Gidoomal's experience as a new follower of Christ could be echoed by many:**

I still remember the awkwardness of my first visit to church - the looking back, nervous, worried about what my friends and family would say. Would they disown me?

Was I betraying my community and culture, by going to what we saw as a Western institution - because for many of us, Jesus Christ was the white man's God. I even pictured him as a city gent, complete with pinstriped suit and bowler hat!

I had become a follower of Christ during my third year reading Physics at Imperial College, London. Although I had been a Christian for several months, I still had not been to a church service. Coming from a Hindu background, I was not sure which church I should go to. Had I become a Protestant or a Catholic? Or a Baptist? Or an Anglican?

It was some months later that I was invited to a worship service in a church. My first instinct when I entered the church building was to remove my shoes, as I had always done before entering a holy place - but everybody else was keeping their shoes on. Then I saw a carpeted area - perfect for sitting on to worship God. I headed towards it, but was directed to wooden pews which were most uncomfortable. And then to top it all, the organ started playing - and I thought, 'My goodness, who's died?' because I associated the organ with funerals. I struggled through the service until the sermon was preached - I was hooked. I came back week after week, just to hear the sermon and suffering through the other bits, but I would make sure to leave without talking to anybody.

*Looking for Directions: Towards an Asian Spirituality,* South Asian Concern, 2006, page 125.

# Reaching out

What then could be the way forward in reaching the large numbers of Buddhists, Hindus, Muslims and Sikhs in Britain? The following comments, from *The New People Next Door*, Lausanne Occasional Paper 55, are still accurate.

> *"Effective evangelism approaches among the South Asian Diaspora communities hardly exist. By and large the host country churches have found it difficult to relate to people of a different culture and established faith and have either given up or left them alone. Work with young people, for example Bible clubs, has been fruitful in a number of countries. Several of today's leaders came to Christ as school or university students. However, for the vast majority of South Asians, Christianity is seen as essentially a part of western culture. Jesus (however greatly they respect him) is the god of white and black people."*[6]

If our aim is for them to see that Jesus Christ is who he claimed to be, then clearly there is a need for new approaches. Here are some:

- **We need to build bridges of friendship and relationship**

It is important to take the time and trouble to do this. It is both an expression of service and a step towards building relationships of trust. In other words it is a mark of our love, as well as justice. It generally involves finding common concerns that are relevant to all communities, and working together, for example

---

6 Lausanne Committee for World Evangelization, *The New People Next Door*, Lausanne Occasional Paper 55 p51

in projects relating to young people or dealing with discrimination, racism, local issues, leisure activities and so on. It requires time to get to know people and what they believe in order to get behind the stereotypes.[7]

- **We need to find ways of working with families and groups rather than only individuals.**

This includes encouraging people to remain within their community and culture, as far as possible, when they follow Christ. Too often individuals have been cut off:

*"When I began to follow Christ it was like a huge bomb being set off in my family. My mother said that the family were being punished because my father had failed to perform certain prayers for his dead parents. Blaming him didn't go down too well, as you can imagine! They feared that it would have a detrimental effect on my sister's marriage prospects. They were also concerned for my welfare because they were aware of Christian cults. There was plenty of emotional blackmail, as I was repeatedly told that I would drive them to a premature death… I became quite cut off from the family, for several years."[8]*

The pressure may come from the family and community. But we should do all we can to help new disciples remain as close to their family as possible. That means allowing them time

---

7   A good example of this is the Near Neighbours programme that was funded by government and operated out of a number of Anglican diocese. The Bradford Churches for Dialogue and Diversity website provides a good insight into this programme - http://www.bcdd.org.uk

8   *Notes for the Journey,* South Asian Concern, 2011, pp. 13, 51

and space, rather than expecting them at church meetings all the time.

**We must develop new forms of church in which people can follow Christ in a way that is open to other members of their community.**

They may use forms of worship and religious language that are appropriate for them. These will of course vary greatly. One example is a group of Gujarati Hindus who meet for a weekly satsang or bhajan group (satsang is a common form of group that meets for singing, prayer or discussion of religious topics). This group is called 'Isu satsang' because its focus is on Isu or Jesus. They sit on the floor, sing and pray in Gujarati.

Over several years a number have become followers of Christ but they do not consider themselves 'Christians'. They know that Christians are generally white (or black) people who go to churches and sit on benches and they do not want to be that. Within their local Gujarati community, which is strongly opposed to 'Christian' culture and ways, and would not want its young people to identify with them, they are accepted, though not without initial suspicions that they were going to be 'converted'.

New Life Suwarta Sangat in Harrow has developed an approach to Gujarati Hindus along similar lines, but with clearer boundaries and a greater mixture of cultures – young people are not the same as their parents.[9]

---

9   www.nlss.org.uk/

One area for creative expression has been festivals. What do Christian believers from Hindu and Sikh backgrounds do at Diwali time? In 1993 a group organised an 'alternative Diwali' at Kensington Temple, a central London church, where they celebrated Jesus as the Light of the World. Others took up the idea. Pall Singh invited people every year to celebrate the Light of the World, usually a week before or after the main Diwali festival, in order not to clash with it. Sunil Kapoor in Nairobi called it the 'Maranatha Festival of Light', avoiding direct connection with Diwali but using the link. For some this is very controversial, for others it is exciting and liberating.

Music is significant. 'Songs of the Kingdom' and 'Asia Worships' were two early albums of fusion music, trying to bridge the gap between generations and music styles, so that people from different backgrounds could join together in their praise and worship.[10] Naujavan[11] has developed newer expressions of fusion.

How do the new and the old churches get on together? Not always very comfortably. Some feel that the traditional ways are good enough, while others are frustrated. What about being known as a 'Christian' or a 'follower of Christ'? Again, there are strong opinions both ways.[12]

---

10  These two albums are now combined as *Celebrating Together,* available along with other 'fusion' albums, from South Asian Concern, PO Box 43, Sutton, Surrey SM2 5WL, UK. info@southasianconcern.org

11  Naujavan is described on their website (http://www.naujavan.com/) as "a movement of young South Asians uniquely made and placed, united as family through the unstoppable love of Jesus. Our mission together is to inspire, develop and equip an emerging generation of South Asians in their Christian walk."

12  These and other issues are examined in *'Notes for the Journey: Following Jesus, Staying South Asian',* South Asian Concern, 2011.

These approaches open up new possibilities. But they also raise big questions. Where are the boundaries? What about baptism and communion? What symbols are appropriate? What about teaching from the Bible? Also, some models are highly focussed on a certain community. It is relevant to them, but only to them. How do you balance concern for one particular group with the truth of the unity and equality of all believers in Christ?

But there is no question that fresh approaches are needed. A good question to ask is 'When people come to Christ, what do you want them to become *culturally*? 'The answers could range from 'White British' to 'Black British' to 'South Asian Islamic/ Hindu' to…? Maybe the best strategy is for new believers to retain their cultural identity at least initially. [13]

## MARG [Making Authentic Relationships Grow]

Timothy Paul, who works with Hindus in the US, has proposed **MARG** as a path of spiritual discovery and gradual acceptance and surrender to the reality of Jesus as the Lord who brings salvation within Hindu culture. He describes five steps in this journey:

*Sabandh/relationship*: building authentic, respectful relationships.

*Anubhav/experience*: experiencing the reality of Jesus through the power of prayer.

*Bhakti/devotion*: joining in worship to Jesus through thanks-giving, singing and prayer.

*Balidan/sacrifice*: learning about the central truth of Jesus' sacrificial death and resurrection.

13  *Notes for the Journey: Following Jesus, Staying south Asian, South Asian concern, 2011*, explores many of these issues

*Sharanam/surrender:* inviting people to surrender to Jesus – without calling them to give up their Hindu heritage.

In this process "it seems that Hindus grow to love Jesus before they come to know him in an exclusive relationship", but in the end he becomes for them "Muktinath, the lord of salvation".[14]

# Iranian churches

The Iranian community is a good example of new believers remaining within their cultural identity. Increasing waves of Iranian asylum seekers have been arriving in the UK since 1995. Many of them are being relocated by the border authorities into towns such as Glasgow, Doncaster, Sheffield, Nottingham and Leeds. Iranian churches have formed in all these areas and provide a community for the new migrants.[15] They often arrive speaking virtually no English and churches provide their only cultural linking group. Mansour Borji leads an Iranian church. He observes that it is difficult for Iranians to assimilate and attend other local churches – mainly because of the language barrier. In order to understand the Bible and Christian teaching they need to learn with a native speaker. However, Iranian churches often benefit very much from partnerships with more established denominations so they can inherit and translate teaching. Borji says: "If the English Church in the local area

---

14 Timothy Paul, *Impacting the Hindu Diaspora in North America*, International Journal of Frontier Missiology, 26:3 Fall 2009 Available at http://www.ijfm.org/PDFs_IJFM/26_3_PDFs/26_3Paul.pdf

15 Some examples of other areas with Iranian Churches include Chiswick, North London, Ealing, Croydon, Sheffield, Bristol, Birmingham, Manchester and Brighton.

knows about the new population then they can contact the Iranians and set up a fellowship that runs as a joint organisation to the local congregation."[16]

## Southampton Lighthouse International Church

The story of Southampton Lighthouse International Church is told in Clive Thorne's book *Light Out of Darkness* [2006].[17] Clive Thorne was trained as a missionary through Operation Mobilisation and his utter dedication to reaching Asians of various religions with the gospel is crucial to the story of the church. He is a wonderful example of loving the lost for Christ's sake. Just as crucial was his partnership with Kudlip Rajo, an Asian believer from a Sikh background, who co-led the fellowship from the beginning.

Though the numbers are not big this work has had considerable success in making disciples for Jesus. It is interesting that in this example becoming culturally more Asian followed conversion and the establishment of a church rather than the other way around. Some of its key characteristics are:

1  A very heavy emphasis on prayer. The progress of the work is bathed in answered prayer and key steps in the work were taken through prophetic words given in the context of prayer.

---

16  Elam churches in Guildford provide a range of resources in Persian.

17  The book by Clive Thorne telling the story of the church can be found on the church's website: www.lighthouseicc.org.uk

2 A passion to share the message of the gospel with an expectation to make converts. At one stage the group were given a target of one convert a month and this was actually fulfilled over many years.

3 Leafleting homes with Christian literature

4 A shop was purchased close to the community where majority world crafts were sold and Christian material in Asian languages was available. This shop did become a meeting place between adherents of the religions and Christians.

5 Clive Thorne visited restaurants where he was able to chat with the staff.

6 Personal testimony that sometimes led to one-to-one Bible study

7 Bible study groups

8 Fellowship meetings on Sunday that eventually led to church. Initially converts would be linked to various churches and meet as a fellowship together on a Sunday afternoon.

9 With increasing numbers more culturally specific provision was made for worshippers with Punjabi/Hindi/Urdu services once a month. As time went on the younger folk in the congregation developed a distinctively young British Asian style of worship that is known as the Naujavan movement.

## St Christopher's, Sparkhill, Birmingham

The Springfield Project based at this church is seen as the main missional expression of the church's life in an area that has a large population of Asian origin. [18]

18 See the church's mission policy at http://www.stchristopherschurch.co.uk/upload/file/Mission_Policy_-_agreed_by_PCC_June_11th_2012.pdf

Over 20 years ago a group of women from St Christopher's Church had a vision to start a stay and play group to support families in the local area.

In May 1999, the Springfield Project was launched, which grew into a community project serving hundreds of families in the Springfield area.

In 2004, Birmingham City Council approached the project to ask if it could become the children's centre for Springfield. Considerable thought was given to this proposal and in 2006 it was agreed that the Springfield Project would deliver Children's Centre services.

Demolishing the church hall made way for a new purpose-built Children's Centre. The project made a financial contribution to the building of the centre to ensure it could accommodate both Children's Centre services, the needs of the project and the church for office space and meeting rooms.

In November 2008, the official opening was conducted by the then Archbishop of Canterbury, Rowan Williams, who was joined by church members, staff, local families and guests from the local mosque.

There are strong and trusted partnerships with Birmingham City Council, local healthcare professionals and The Feast, a charity working to encourage friendships and understanding between Muslims and Christians in local secondary schools.

## Making friends: are there boundaries?

It is inevitable if we become friends with adherents of other religions that we will be invited to participate in events in their lives that will include religious rituals. A simple example would be an invite to be guests at a marriage ceremony. Evangelicals disagree about the extent to which we can feel free to witness the religious rituals of our friends.

One reason for this is the close connection between culture and religion, which we discussed in the previous chapter. How much of a wedding ceremony is cultural and how much religious? A wedding (in any cultural or faith community) is clearly a family occasion with cultural and community traditions, but also has a religious element. Festivals combine both cultural and religious elements. Sometimes it is hard to make the distinction. How do we balance our family obligations with our faith commitment?

There is also a difference between attending an occasion as an observer or guest and participating in the activity. Again the distinctions can be hard to make.

The following quote from the section on festivals on South Asian Concern's website represents one end of the spectrum. The section concerns the Hindu festival of Navaratri:

> "This festival takes place in September or October. Navaratri means nine nights and this is how long the festival lasts. It is celebrated by Hindus from the state of Gujarat in India. They worship the goddess Parvati, the wife of Shiva. In the home they place a small brass image of her on a bed of rice in a copper dish and perform puja before it twice a day... In this country during Navaratri some Hindu families get together each night in a local hall to enjoy singing devotional songs in praise of the goddess and dancing stick dances, known as raas garba. These are folk dances in which people knock short sticks together to keep time. They dance round a

*special shrine to Parvati. This is a six-sided box with a cone-shaped top. On the top is a lamp, and on each side of the box there is a picture of a different goddess. The whole thing is decorated with coloured lights and tinsel. During the evening a priest performs the arati ceremony. Lots of brass maps are placed around the shrine and people make offerings of fruit and sweets. These are later given out as prasad."*

In large cities in Britain the dances are often organised by a small group of people who hire a hall and musicians and then sell tickets for the event, known as a garba night.

At the end of the description of this and other festivals there are some things to do:

1  Ask a Hindu friend to tell you which festivals they celebrate and why.

2  Find out the dates of the local Hindu festivals. Ask if you may visit, most Hindus will be delighted that you want to do this.

3  A few days before the festival ask about the story behind it and find out what the worshipers do.'[19]

There is no suggestion here that witnessing the Navaratri dances that are clearly a part of idolatrous worship would be a problem for Christians. Neither is there any suggestion as to how Christians should respond if they are offered Prasad – the fruit and sweets that have been offered to the goddess.

A different view is expressed by C.K.Mody in his *Empty and Evil: the worship of other faiths in 1 Corinthians 8-10 and today*[20].

---

19 http://southasianconcern.org/south-asians/hindu-sikh-festivals/

20 C.K.Mody in his *Empty and Evil: the worship of other faiths in 1 Corinthians 8-10 and today*, London: Latimer Trust, 2010

Mody, a convert from Zoroastrianism, deals with a number of pastoral scenarios in light of his study of 1 Corinthians 8-10. None fit exactly the case of attending the Navaratri dances but we can extrapolate his likely advice from the cases he considers. One case is an invitation to attend a Sikh wedding. Mody argues that because doing so would involve attending a gurdwara where guests would be expected to wear a head covering out of respect to the Sikh god, that the invitation should be refused. He bases his opinion on consideration for the weaker brother/sister in the case of eating foods offered to idols discussed by Paul in 1 Corinthians 8:7-13. Another case is being offered sweets at a dinner in a Hindu friend's house where the host explains that the sweets have been offered to their gods – are *prasad*. He advises refusal in light of Paul's teaching in 1 Corinthians 10:28-29.

It seems that the approach of South Asian Concern takes seriously the biblical position that idolatry has no foundation in reality while Mody focuses on the link between idolatry and the demonic. As we saw in the previous chapter, both truths are part of the complex reality of the gods behind the images. As Paul's discussion in 1 Corinthians 8-10 shows, each case has to be judged on its merits and each person's situation is different, depending also on their relationships – with the people of the other faith and with their fellow believers.[21]

To respect both truths is clearly not always easy. But to love our religious other neighbour as ourselves must ultimately be conditioned by our love of God who is Father, Son and Holy Spirit.

---

21  There is a full discussion of these issues, with case studies, in *Notes for the Journey*, London, South Asian Concern, 2011, pages 51-60

# Conclusion

Much of this chapter has tried to convey what Christian love looks like in the context of reaching out with the gospel to adherents of the religions. From the perspective of a comfortable Western lifestyle to love our religious neighbour seems very challenging. But if we prefer the perspective of the self-sacrificing love of Jesus it becomes a privilege. The intensity of the challenge or privilege is dependent on proximity. It is now almost impossible to avoid contact with people from the religions in the UK but living among them in an inner city is very different to the occasional contact elsewhere. But we all have a gospel responsibility towards the people from many nations that have come to live among us.

**One thing that we can all do is pray the news.** A Tearfund supporter alerted me to this possibility. Every time she saw a news report that showed the suffering of the poor, she prayed. It would be just as easy to pray every time we see or hear a news report that refers to the religions. More often than not reports with a religious reference will refer to Islam – especially Islamic extremism or terrorism. We can pray for their victims; we can pray that their eyes will be opened to the truth of the gospel; we can pray that the Muslim community will be protected from the hate that extremists generate; we can pray that extremist action will make many Muslims more willing to hear the message about Jesus.

Jesus had compassion on the crowds because they were harassed and helpless like sheep without a shepherd but he also saw the same crowds as a harvest field that needed workers to gather the harvest in.[22] We need to pray that God will raise evangelists to go with the good news of the kingdom to the people of the

---

22  Matthew 9:35-38.

religions. Throughout the history of the Church there have been outstanding evangelists like Paul but most evangelists have been ordinary people that for various reasons have moved into an area and gossiped the gospel.

**What is needed is for many to move to live where the religions are concentrated as intentional missional communities – and the most effective evangelists in this context would be those from the community that have become disciples of Jesus. There is also a need to equip Christians that respond to this call.**

Living among people of the religions requires sensitivity and understanding. Encounter is more than likely to begin in a fog of mutual prejudice. We may need to take deliberate actions, such as giving up alcohol, to prove that being Christian and Western are not synonymous. The idea of conversion can be difficult for Hindus and Sikhs to accept because it can be seen as requiring them to abandon their communities. Consequently, it may be necessary to find more innovative ways of talking about salvation.

**In short, reaching out to adherents of the religions requires that we deliberately change our lifestyle in order to diminish the barriers that hinder our friends from hearing the gospel.**

We must also realise that our communal worship culture will be very alien to people from the religions. The simpler the worship the easier it will be. The house church model with discussion over a meal or small group Bible study is probably most effective. With growth more formal churches in particular will need to think in terms of multi-lingual and multi-cultural worship services. [23]

23  St James' Alperton is a good example of an evangelical Anglican church that has become multi-lingual and multi-cultural to accomodate people from the religions - http://www.stjamesalperton.org.uk/home

Making friends is central in any attempt to attract people from the religions to become disciples of Jesus. What is in view here is not a technique for making disciples but a genuine love for people.

**The religious stranger we may befriend should never be given any grounds to suspect that our friendship is conditional on their becoming followers of Jesus. Loving for Christ's sake is unconditional love.**

There may however be limits to our friendship. Friendship with someone from another religion is very likely to lead to invitations to participate in events that are important to our friends in which religious rituals are performed. It is very difficult to legislate on what one can and cannot do in the very varied circumstances that may arise. The conscience of the weaker brother or sister may be relevant on some occasions.

# CHAPTER 4
# Pastoral issues[1]

Given what was said about conversion in the last chapter it may be wise to look for different terminology. However precious the language of 'conversion' has been to us as evangelicals and without minimising in any way the momentous step that is taken when someone converts, there are more sensitive ways to describe what has happened. We can use other words such as 'new disciples', or speak of 'turning to Christ' rather than 'conversion'. Similarly we may refer to these new disciples as 'followers of Jesus/Christ' or 'believers in Jesus/Christ' rather than 'Christians'. 'Christian' is a word with many connotations that are mainly cultural rather than spiritual for people from the religions. Many equate becoming a 'Christian' with adopting the lax morality of Western society.

## The 'insider movement' in the UK

Believing that joining a UK church would mean a decisive break with their own community and culture there are those that are becoming disciples of Jesus in the UK that are choosing to remain within their cultural tradition. Some pastors and missionaries in communities where there are many adherents of

---

1   This section is substantially based on Kate Wharton's unpublished paper *From Conversion to Maturity: Guidelines on Caring for Converts to Christianity from Other Faiths*

the religions also accept that becoming a disciple of Jesus may not lead to joining a Western type of church. Some missionaries even believe that it is better for some converts not to join a church in their locality.

The idea that a new believer can follow Jesus while going to the mosque for prayer or observing certain Hindu rituals is clearly controversial among evangelicals. It is worth quoting the whole of the section on this matter in the Cape Town Commitment. This was the statement issued by the most representative gathering of evangelicals ever held under the banner of the Lausanne Movement:

> *"So called 'insider movements' are to be found within several religions. These are groups of people who are now following Jesus as their God and Saviour. They meet together in small groups for fellowship, teaching, worship and prayer centred around Jesus and the Bible while continuing to live socially and culturally within their birth communities, including some elements of its religious observance. This is a complex phenomenon and there is much disagreement over how to respond to it. Some commend such movements. Others warn of the danger of syncretism. Syncretism, however, is a danger found among Christians everywhere as we express our faith within our own cultures. We should avoid the tendency, when we see God at work in unexpected or unfamiliar ways, either (i) hastily to classify it and promote it as a new mission strategy, or (ii) hastily to condemn it without sensitive contextual listening."[2]*

In the spirit of Barnabas who, on arrival in Antioch, "saw the evidence of the grace of God" and "was glad and encouraged

---

2   The full Cape Town Commitment can be read at https://www.lausanne.org/content/ctc/ctcommitment (accessed 3/11/2016)

them all to remain true to the Lord", (Acts 11:20-24) we would appeal to all those who are concerned with this issue to:

1  Take as their primary guiding principle the apostolic decision and practice: 'We should not make it difficult for the Gentiles who are turning to God.' (Acts 15:19)

2  Exercise humility, patience and graciousness in recognising the diversity of viewpoints, and conduct conversations without stridency and mutual condemnation. (Romans 14:1-3)

## Appreciating the significance of conversion

Yet an increasing number are becoming disciples of Jesus and joining UK churches. However sudden or gradual the turning towards Jesus is, the turning also implies identification with churches with their roots firmly embedded in the British Christian tradition. So, this chapter deals with what these Christian communities and their leaders need to be and do in embracing converts from the religions.

The first thing we need to do when someone from the religions seeks to join our church fellowship as a disciple of Christ is to appreciate the seriousness of the step being taken. My mother was a true disciple of Jesus and went to be with the Lord when I was 10. Five years later I experienced an evangelical conversion and became passionate about my faith to the dismay of my nominally Christian non-conformist father. If conversion can create tension and outrage in a nominally Christian family then the impact on a devout Hindu or Muslim family can be multiplied a hundredfold.

It is right to rejoice when a mother bringing her child to the church mother and toddler group wants to know more about what it means to follow Jesus or a friend in work wants to meet to read and discuss passages from the New Testament – but when they start talking about being disciples of Jesus or con-verting it is important to realise how big a step they are taking.

When a church in the UK welcomes a new believer from a Bud-dhist, Hindu, Jewish, Muslim or Sikh background they may not be familiar with the politics surrounding conversion within their community. This kind of knowledge is not necessary in order to share the gospel but is essential to understanding some of the family situations with which a new believer may have to cope. Without such understanding the church is ill-prepared to care for and support new believers from the religions.

Welcoming new believers has always been the main pur-pose and calling of the Church. The fact that many believers are now from different cultural backgrounds should not be seen as problematic or something to cause anxiety, but as the beginning of more credible Christian witness to an increasingly mixed society.

## The importance of hospitality

*"If anyone comes to me and does not hate his father and mother, his wife and children, his brothers and sisters - yes, even his own life - he cannot be my disciple."* (Luke 14:26)

It is when we consider the implications of conversion for adher-ents of the religions that we realise how important it is for the church to be the loving and welcoming 'family' that it was meant to be. Becoming followers of Jesus often means loss of family at least temporarily and the need for an alternative family is acute.

Each new believer who is rejected by their family needs a new family. They need more than one person to be there for them.

To fulfil this role it's important that churches are familiar with the context of new believers so that they can see things from their perspective and be family for them. What new believers lose in following Jesus can be very significant. This loss needs to be healed through the love of their new church community/family and its faithfulness.

## Understanding a new believer's background

Any conversion, even from a secular background, involves leaving your old life behind, along with your old friends and priorities. For a new believer whose community is hostile to Christianity this sense of loss-of-bearings is increased.

Any sense of community is built up by spending a lot of time in each other's houses or together at home. Kuldip Rajo at the Southampton Lighthouse fellowship has explained this with reference to funerals. When a member of a family that you know by name but not really very well dies, you probably would not take the whole day off to go and sit with them. However, this would be the natural response of someone from a South Asian background. This kind of time generosity is also needed just to keep in touch with all aunts, uncles and cousins.

Community ties are not just social they are also economic. Immigrant communities build business networks because they face racism and class disadvantage trying to compete in the UK. If the new believer has a profession or is highly educated then they are likely to be financially independent, but if they work in a family business, conversion could have a negative effect not only on their own working life but also their relative's deals. This kind of direct causal effect on loved ones is often one of the main reasons for reversion - to protect family from harm.

## Honour/shame culture

In order to understand new believers from a Muslim, Hindu or Sikh background it is useful to know about honour/shame culture. This culture is not directly connected to any specific religion and is spread throughout the globe, from Mediterranean areas such as Cyprus, to Africa, Central and South America and Asia.

In an honour/shame culture, a family's honour is related to their longstanding reputation for producing moral, trustworthy sons and daughters. Honour is the earned right to make good partnerships both in marriage and business. In an honour culture, the fear of public disgrace is very strong. Women often are seen as the bearers of honour, and chastity upholds the family's reputation. Conversion (like getting pregnant outside of marriage) brings shame on the whole family. It can result in siblings being rejected for marriages.

In the process of conversion there are various crisis or trigger points when a family's sense of shame increases. The first obvious crisis is the moment of confession of a change of faith. This should be handled as gradually as possible and treated at first as a purely internal affair. Many new believers may choose to remain permanently partially hidden, only known to be followers of Christ by one sibling or one parent.

A second crisis point occurs when the new believer decides that they want to declare their new faith publicly. In honour/shame culture, there is no dishonour or humiliation if the fault remains concealed. The family may exert a lot of pressure to ensure that the new believer continues to live outwardly as a Muslim or Sikh. If the news gets out then the family may punish the believer in order to show the community they are doing something to purge the shame.

The third major crisis point is baptism. Someone who becomes a follower of Jesus from Islam may not be ready for baptism for a long time. Historically, in the early Christian centuries believers often waited till towards the end of their lives before they were baptised. For a believer from another faith baptism may likewise need to be something saved for full maturity. It is very important that no pressure is applied by Christian mentors.

## Identity

Young people from the second or third generation (after immigration) can grow up with a split identity, caught in between two communities. Some find that this identity crisis resolves as Christian conversion gives them a new sense of integrity. Others find that conversion causes a more severe split, as they feel divided from half of themselves, in going against their community. In Islam the communal reinforcement of faith, through shared prayer actions and shared recitation, is very strong. The new follower of Christ may feel that their identity was formed and reinforced by this group dynamic and they may find it hard to develop a sense of their new Christian identity without regular ritual attendance. Others may see their new identity as a rejection of all their previous practices. Sometimes the assertion of a new identity can become too aggressive. Mazhar Mallouhi describes how he denigrated his Muslim background and tried "even to embody Zionism". This resulted in an identity struggle because he felt he was betraying his Syrian roots. He eventually resolved to call himself 'culturally' a Muslim and 'spiritually' a Christ follower. This could be judged to be a dual identity, but that is the reality for people that have moved from one religion to another: they want to affirm their cultural heritage, which is closely linked to their former religious community, while embracing their new spiritual identity in Christ. Many rules and regulations for 'Christian' behaviour are part of European cultural norms that do not have to be adopted by followers of Christ from another cultural background. The discussion of contextualisation generated by the insider movement could help in encouraging converts in this context.

## Different forms of Islam, Hinduism and Sikhism

Islam, Hinduism and Sikhism contain many diverse cultures within them. It is important to gain knowledge about each individual's specific background. Some new believers may be 'nominal' Muslims, others may be Sufis or members of Sufi influenced 'post-islamist' movements like Mihaj ul'Qur'an. Among the Sunni majority, Deobandi schools are usually seen as more conservative, Barelvi schools as more moderate. Only four per cent of British Muslims are Shia, but by far the largest groups of Christ followers from Islam are ex-Shia, from the Iranian community.

Religious denomination is often connected to caste, clan and guilds. Within Hinduism different castes may worship different gods or gurus. Many Hindu groups in the UK are new religious movements that have developed over the last two centuries. These new traditions are highly inclusive and membership is often due to a choice of conversion rather than a long-established lineage connection or caste-identity.[3] Contemporary Hinduism has redefined itself as based on an all-encompassing, pluralist spirituality. Converts from Hinduism often contest the exclusivity of Christian salvation and continue to believe 'all religions are one'. Many view Christ as just one avatar among many. Again the question is raised of where the dividing line is between the convert's previous religious identity and new

---

3    For example Sai Baba and ISKCON.

Christian identity. Many may say 'I am a Hindu but I love Christ.' They will be reluctant to change their cultural identification and standing within their community, and therefore will keep their response to the gospel private rather than openly converting. For many Hindus their journey to Christ is a gradual process of growing understanding, based on an initial attraction to Christ without realising the implications of his lordship and unique demands.[4]

There is also a range of cultural practices from beginning tasks on an astrologically auspicious day to rules of purification that may continue to influence a new believer.

## Care and support of new believers

### Ask us: don't assume

It is important to listen very carefully to a new believer's story at the beginning. It may not be right to put them automatically into an Alpha Course, for instance, because so much of the course is about the question of the existence of God. For most new believers from other religions, the existence of God is not an issue. The new believer should be given an individually tailored programme of introduction and welcome; overseen by a hand-picked mentor and a four or five person support group. It is important not to make them feel like a 'guinea pig' but to develop the programme with them. Visit them at home or invite them to your home. If their English is weak they may need a few months of very basic conversation classes first. They may need someone to stand with them in church and work through the order of service, hymns and Bible readings. It

4   For an expansion of this topic see Robin Thomson, *Engaging with Hindus,* The Good Book Company, 2014, pp 114-115

would also be useful to find a Christian mentor who can speak to them in their own language.

If the new believer is comfortable speaking in English, it may be useful to begin by asking them what they were brought up to believe about Christianity. One Hindu said to me that he had seen Christianity as a murderous religion because it involved eating flesh and drinking wine. He said that only the esoteric tantric rituals would use such substances in India.

New believers interviewed in preparing guidelines for the Church of England asked that the church that first welcomes them should gradually help them find the form of worship that suits them best. They should be encouraged to visit a range of churches and experience a range of services with a mentor. Some religions have the same compulsive form of service everywhere so a new believer may not be aware of the diversity of Christian services. Some new believers find this diversity quite confusing, but this is better than them judging the whole by only part of the spectrum. It is important that new believers don't miss out on finding the right place where they feel they really fit in. The first church may be the right receiving centre for them but it may not be the place they settle. They need, like adopted children, to find the right new family.'

## Culturally inclusive church

If a new believer or group of them settles in your area, then there are a number of opportunities to involve the wider congregation in the process of welcoming them. It is an excuse to open up a debate about 'Britishness' and church life. The congregation may wish to try new ways of worshipping to make believers from other cultural backgrounds welcome such as singing a hymn in Tamil or Urdu or inviting a band using South Asian instruments to teach Christian Bhajans (devotional songs).[5]

Learn the cultural distribution of your area by checking the Census or contacting the local authority and if there are a large group of Gujaratis or Somalis then have some Bibles, prayer books and other materials ready in the right languages. Visiting churches that have a majority South Asian or Middle Eastern congregation may provide ideas for new worship structures, such as the Iranian Christian Community in Chiswick or St James, Alperton.

There are several stumbling blocks for new believers that are commonly recognised: the wearing of revealing clothing in church, informal treatment of the Bible (such as placing it on the floor), the wearing of shoes in church, the sitting together of men and women. Some converts don't like to be touched or hugged by members of the opposite sex when they share the peace.

Each new believer needs to be asked their sensitivities relating to meat/pork eating, alcohol consumption and other issues that may affect hospitality. It may be wise to always provide a vegetarian option in a church with Hindu background believers.[6] The aversion to alcohol amongst Hindus, Sikhs and Muslims is very strong and the relaxed attitude of most parishes towards its consumption often scandalises them.

Most new believers interviewed said that feeling welcome was not necessarily to do with the church changing its culture, but more to do with love. They felt that if genuine love and care

---

5    Cf. Material in Chapter 3 p. 68.

6    Robin Thomson op. cit. p. 110.

was given to them then they could adapt and fit in with the structures and habits of church life.

## When to tell the family?

There are such complex consequences to conversion from other religions that it is important to be very cautious in deciding when a new follower of Jesus should tell their family. It could easily be presumed that this is one of the first and most basic steps in becoming a disciple but in certain circumstances it can be advisable to delay any public announcement for an extended amount of time. At the very least how and when to talk to family should be discussed with new believers as a matter of priority. Especially for those from a Muslim background experience suggests that the new believers that developed the best long-term relationship with their family were those that took the longest to tell them. He suggests that it is best for the new believer to attain some maturity as a Christ follower so he or she can cope better with the family's response.

Some evangelists argue that it is better for a new believer to cut themselves off from their family on conversion as this lessens the risk of reversion. However, others argue that it is better for them to stay living with their family so the two worlds don't bifurcate.

Despite some problems new believers should be encouraged to know that relationships with families do generally improve over time.

## From conversion to maturity

It is good to help those that have trusted in Jesus from a life characterised by a daily routine of prayer or ritual to be helped into a daily routine of Christian prayer and worship. For individuals there are books of daily prayer, Bible readings and devotional comment that can be recommended. For families there are aids for daily family devotions.[7] Mentors and small groups can also meet with a new believer regularly for encouragement and prayer.

Like any other new believer those from the religions also need to be encouraged to become familiar with the 'form of sound words' of biblical teaching – through individual study, corporate Bible studies and listening to sermons.

All new believers have very high expectations. Christ promised them "life and life in abundance".[8] Most will go through some phases when the church they are attending or the church leadership disappoints them. They may feel lonely or disillusioned. Sometimes it can be important to encourage them to take on more responsibilities and leadership roles, so they share the burden of creating a spiritual environment in which they can flourish. The energy of responsibility can bring services to life in a new way.

Some new believers may go through a phase where they doubt or lose their faith. If people decide to revert or back out of their Christian commitments they should still be supported emotionally. Relationships should be maintained without judgment and in a spirit of understanding.

## Asylum seekers

Many asylum seekers are joining church congregations in the UK with the inevitable consequence that the church is drawn

---

7   Daily family devotions was once standard practice among evangelicals and needs to be resurrected.

8   John 10:10

into accompanying them in the complex process of seeking asylum. With asylum law and the regulations that go with it being in a constant state of flux because of government pre-occupation with the level of immigration this is an area where specialist advice is essential.

For example, the recent Methodist guidelines on support-ing asylum cases observe that the Home Office can question whether certain denominations are evangelical or non-evan-gelical. They may then proceed to argue that a Christian of the non-evangelical denomination may safely return to their coun-try of origin, as they are not in danger if they do not announce their faith or seek to be an evangelist.[9]

With the law and its regulations constantly changing, seek-ing the advice of a lawyer who specialises in immigration law should be the first step. This can be supplemented by view-ing information that's freely available online. For example the Methodist guidelines are available at:

www.methodist.org.uk/mission/asylum-and-immigration

The following websites are also useful:

www.refugee-action.org.uk/get_help_advice/ asylum_advice

www.gov.uk/browse/visas-immigration/asylum

www.gov.uk/claim-asylum/overview

www.asylumaid.org.uk/the-asylum-process-made-simple

........................................................................................................................

9    Asylum Applications and Christian belief.
     www.methodist.org.uk/downloads/pi_mins_asylum_briefing1905.doc

# Marriage

When Tom Walsh interviewed 16 UK-based Muslim background believers in depth he found that by far the majority of stabilised, mature believers had married Christians. But meeting members of the other sex and forming a relationship is a very difficult matter for an individual who has been brought up in gendered segregation and expecting their marriage to be arranged. Both men and women struggle with this and speak of their frustration in not finding a Christian partner (when community ties would have ensured they could marry easily if they had not converted). Some churches run singles events and the idea of a closed website for networking could be a helpful development. More mature fellow believers need to be conscious of this issue and of the possibility that they could help in introducing new believers to possible marriage partners.

## *Inter-marriage*

The 2001 Census revealed that there were nearly 22,000 inter-religious marriages in England, Wales and Scotland. Recognising that such marriages can only become more common the Christian-Muslim Forum published guidelines entitled *When Two Faiths Meet, Marriage, Family and Pastoral Care* to address the issue in November 2012. The case studies in this resource indicate that the religious adherence of at least one of the partners in most inter-religious marriages is nominal. This suggests that it is not something that will be encountered often in evangelical churches. However, counselling and support may be required in at least three areas:

1  A church member contemplating marrying someone from another religion.

2  A convert from a religion who is already married.

3  A parent whose child has married someone from another religion and whose grandchildren are being raised in that religion.

## 1. A church member contemplating marrying someone from another religion

2 Corinthians 6:14-7:1 is a key text for church leaders in guiding a member who may be contemplating marrying someone from another religion. Marriage is not specifically mentioned in this passage. Women and many men in New Testament times would not have had an option where their marriage partner was concerned. However, in our society where both women and men are free to choose their marriage partner the strong advice not to be so closely associated with unbelievers so that one could be drawn to compromise with idolatry is clearly relevant.

As described by Paul in Ephesians 5 the marriage of two Christians has the potential of amazing benefits for both woman and man. A Christian man or woman entering into marriage with someone that is not only a non-believer in Jesus but a believer in another god would be denying themselves these benefits.

An important consideration for a Christian contemplating it would be the religious upbringing of any children from the union. A Muslim family is very likely to insist that any children should be raised as Muslims. There would be less pressure from Hindu or Sikh families but there could be pressure in their case as well. Obviously leaders cannot force an individual's conscience but the implications for any children of marrying someone from another religion should be made clear to anyone contemplating marrying someone from another religion.

In the event of advice not to marry being ignored, the Christian should be supported in every way possible. Continuing contact with the church should be encouraged and every effort made to welcome the non-Christian partner.

Since more than 60 per cent of regular church attendees are women, the pressure for women to marry outside the faith can be intense. With the increase of believers from other religions in the community it is possible for this issue to arise more frequently in the future.

## 2. A new believer who is already married

Much of what has been said about the care of new believers in this chapter is relevant to those that are married. What is in focus here is the impact of the conversion on the new believer's marriage and how to support them through what could be serious consequences for their marriage. The key scripture in this case is 1 Corinthians 7:12-14.

Marriage is a creation ordinance so does not depend on whether both partners believe the same. So the conversion of one partner does not annul the marriage. Paul recommends that as long as the non-Christian partner is content to stay with the Christian partner there should be no separation. The Christian should do everything in her/his power to keep the marriage intact with the hope of seeing the unbelieving partner turning to Jesus. But if the non-Christian partner is not content to stay in the marriage then separation and divorce is allowed. Married converts should, therefore, be encouraged to stay in their marriages and be supported to do so in every way possible.

Paul does not say that a new follower of Christ should stay with an unbelieving partner regardless of their reaction to the partner's conversion. Being 'willing to live' with the Christian partner includes accepting the conversion and continuing to love and respect the converted party. Being 'willing to stay' means being able to live in peace together (verse 5). If the unbelieving partner becomes abusive towards the converted partner then that is clear evidence of an unwillingness to stay and the converted partner should be encouraged to recognise the end of the marriage and be supported through separation.

### 3. A parent whose child has married someone from another religion and whose grandchildren are being raised in that religion

Freedom to convert from one religion to another is a fundamental human right. Even so, to see a child turn their back on God can be a painful experience for any parent. To see them convert to another religion and bring up their children in that religion is doubly painful. There is also the possibility that a child's husband/wife agree to marry on condition that any children should be raised in their religion. Parents and grandparents in such circumstances will need much wisdom, prayer and support.

## The use of church buildings

There is a wide spectrum of views among evangelicals about the significance of church buildings. On one end of the spectrum is the belief that a building is sanctified by the worship that goes on in it. The building itself, because consecrated to God, is a holy place and is qualitatively different from other buildings that are not consecrated for the purpose of worship. Added to this the furniture in such buildings is also holy – especially those associated with aspects of worship such as the altar/communion table, candles etc. Other artefacts such as stained glass windows and pictures/icons can also become holy.

At the other end of the spectrum is the belief that a building can never be holy in and of itself. Underlying this conviction is the belief that God as a result of the new covenant established through Jesus Christ resides in His people. The Church is the gathered people of God and the building where they meet is just a meeting place and nothing more. This is why many evangelicals have no problem meeting in theatres, lecture rooms, schools, abandoned factories, warehouses etc. Evangelicals with this conviction also meet in buildings that have been used for worship for many years – sometimes centuries. They value that history but the fabric of the building and its contents remain just fabric. The moment God's people leave the building it is no holier than the pub, offices, car park or whatever other building there is adjacent to it.

The conviction that buildings are not holy has probably been a factor in the massive increase by evangelicals in making their buildings available for community use although the key factor is probably the growing belief in integral mission. In many cases churches receive public funding to make their buildings more suited to community use as well as to run community activities. When this happens the question whether there should be any limit on community use often arises. This becomes particularly acute when a request is made to use the building by religious groups or groups whose activities have religious undertones.

An example would be a request to run yoga classes. Yoga was developed as a meditation technique in the Hindu and Buddhist traditions. Some argue that the physical and mental aspects of yoga can be divorced from its original religious formation while others deny that this is possible. But even if this is possible the way yoga is promoted as a way of creating a peace in the human heart that is ultimately only achieved through knowing God is fundamentally religious.

Another example would be a request to use the building for an explicitly religious activity such as Buddhist meditation or to celebrate a Hindu festival. Some would be unhappy about letting the building for such activities because in the public's mind the church building is associated with the Christian faith. Seeing groups from another religion using the 'Christian' building, it is argued, would confuse them or confirm the very common public perception that all religions are ultimately about the same reality anyway. This argument that people outside the church would be confused fits in well with the belief that the building used by the church is holy. However, if the church has received public funding to make the buildings fit for public use the church's policy for letting the building should be agreed with the funder. Without such an agreement the church could lay itself open to a charge of discrimination. A church would do well to seek legal advice when entering into such a contract.

In negotiations with funders churches may have to face some challenging issues. For example, an authority may insist that their support requires that the building be devoid of any evidence that it is a place of Christian worship when in public use. This would mean removing crosses, altar, banners etc. Some evangelicals who believe that buildings and their paraphernalia are holy would see this as compromising their faith for the sake of public funding. Others, who believe that God's presence is made manifest in His people, would be happy to remove Christian material objects as long as believers are present in the service offered to the community.

The effective use of church buildings for the community depends a great deal on the relationship between the church and the community. In areas where there is a concentration of adherents of the religions, community relations is about relations with people who belong to the religions. The experience of Christian community service that has been gained through Christian development agencies like Tearfund has proven beyond doubt that service *with* the community is always more effective than service for. This means dialogue with the community. So, where the church desires to bless its community the best strategy is to talk to the people and work alongside them. Churches that have gone down this route have found that it is very important for the church to be very upfront about its faith. In that context they are able to make their buildings available and welcome many people from the religions into their premises.

**Narthex Centre, Sparkhill, Birmingham**
Narthex Centre is a faith-based charity set up by St John's Anglican Church in Sparkhill. The heart of Narthex's work is to meet the culturally diverse needs of our local communities, providing quality facilities that offer a place of welcome. It works in one of the four per cent most deprived communities in the UK, with the second highest area of children under five living in poverty. Sparkhill Parish is 93 per cent ethnic minority residents with the highest group being Asian Muslim. Against this backdrop of need and diversity the Narthex Centre seeks to fulfil its' mandate of 'Encouraging Cohesion' through education, social action, families, children's and young people's work.

## Using a church building for inter-religious worship

What is in view here is a service where readings, songs and prayers from various religious traditions are used. The conceptual root of the idea of inter-religious worship is twofold:

### 1) The concept of civic religion

Historically, the state has more often than not sought the approval of religion to bolster its authority. The Anglican settlement in England in the reign of Queen Elizabeth I married the state very closely to a particular ecclesiastical structure. This survived fully until 1689 and remnants of it are still with us – the most obvious being the presence of bishops in parliament and the coronation ritual. But even in countries like the US where church and state are strictly separated religion plays its part in civic ritual, such as the prayers that are offered at the inauguration of the president. What these rituals do is provide an endorsement for public officials and elected officials from a religious community. It is not surprising, therefore that officials seek religious endorsement at the local as well as the national level. Where the community is made up of a number of religions there is sometimes a presumption that endorsement should be sought from the various religions. This is where the inter-religious service is born. But the possibility of thoroughly inter-religious services needs a theology of religious pluralism. Some clergy have come to espouse this theology.

### 2) A theology of religious pluralism

Religious pluralism is the belief that the ultimate reality encountered in the various religions is one. A typical, clichéd metaphor is the many paths to the top of a mountain. Another is blind men encountering an elephant – one blind man bumps into the elephant's leg and says that the creature is like a tree; another gets hold of the trunk and says that it's like a pipe; another gets hold of the tail and says that it's like a rope. The ways the elephant is described are very different but they are actually describing the same animal. This is not the place for a detailed critique of the theology of religious pluralism. However, the metaphor of the elephant actually comes from the Indian religious tradition that sees the material as ultimately unreal. To find ultimate reality is to escape the clutches of embodied existence – for the Hindu by absorption into the divine and for the Buddhist by putting out the embodied fire of suffering. Interestingly liberal Christianity made possible the endorsement of this Eastern approach when it cut the cord that held history and faith together. For those in the Semitic religious tradition, i.e. the Jewish, Christian, Muslim and Sikh, the belief that God intervenes in history and that the revelation of His being and what He demands from human beings has been communicated in authoritative words is axiomatic. So, when what the religions say about god is taken seriously it is simply not possible to conclude that it is the same god that is being worshipped in the various religions.

**To imply, as inter-religious services do, that the religions are equally valid ways to the ultimate reality is actually a profound insult to the intelligence and piety of people that are serious about their religion.**

Serious Christians, like serious Muslims, Jews or Sikhs, would not want to be involved in inter-religious services with even a hint of approving religious pluralism. This has nothing to do with tolerance. Tolerance is to respect those that differ from us. To say that we are actually ignorant of the essence of our cherished religions as the theology of religious pluralism does is the ultimate intolerance.

We should graciously refuse to have anything to do with inter-religious services.

As for providing some sort of civic affirmation of elected officials if we have good relations with the various religious groups in our community it should not be beyond us to devise some means to do this that does not involve inter-religious worship. Members of the religions would be more than happy, with non-religious civil society groups, to attend a reception in a neutral venue to welcome an official. Many religious people from different traditions would also be happy to welcome officials to their buildings and to pray for the official in their unique way.[10]

## Conclusion

**In light of the antipathy of the religions to concepts such as 'convert', 'conversion' or 'Christian' – that the secular world also shares to a certain extent – it may be better to use terms such as 'new believer' and 'becoming/being a follower/disciple of Jesus Christ'.**

That there is an insider movement in the UK should be a cause for rejoicing. Rather than be suspicious of those that become disciples of Jesus while choosing to remain within their cultural identity we should pray that God will lead them by His Spirit

---

10  For a fuller discussion of this topic see David Bookless, *Interfaith Worship and Christian Faith*, Grove Books, 1991

into all truth and use them to introduce many in their community to Jesus as Lord and Saviour.

We should appreciate that for someone from one of the religions to choose to identify with a historic church in the UK is a very big step that is likely to have serious ramifications in their life. It is possible that the church will need to be the family that they have lost. Maybe what the Church in the UK needs is an influx of new believers from the religions to undermine the ungodly individualism that is very prevalent among us.

**To welcome new believers from the religions properly will require a good understanding of their religious background. This may mean understanding not only their Buddhist/Hindu/Muslim background in general but the specific group or sect that they come from.**

The cultures of the religions are generally more focused on honour/shame than Western culture that is more focused on guilt/justice. We may need to appreciate that the God of the Bible that we have traditionally viewed through the lens of guilt/justice can without contradiction also be viewed through the lens of honour/shame. We may learn to see the glory/honour of God more fully as we pastor new believers from an honour/shame culture.

We should rejoice at the cultural diversity that new believers from minority ethnic communities could create in our churches. All believers love to worship in their heart language/mother tongue.

**Churches should be happy to cater for multi-lingual and multi-cultural worship. For the church to model unity in diversity would be a wonderful example of what is possible in society at large.**

Marriage in a multi-religious context is creating a number of new and complex pastoral challenges:

- A new believer from a background of arranged marriages may need help in finding a marriage partner.

- Pastors are more likely to encounter couples from different religions wanting to marry. Such couples should be alerted to the unique difficulties encountered in such marriages. In some evangelical churches entering into a mixed marriage would be seen as direct disobedience to the Bible and a matter for church discipline.

- A new believer whose partner chooses to remain as an adherent of one of the religions will need special support.

- The upbringing of children is a particularly challenging issue in mixed marriages. Parents and grandparents may need a lot of support to negotiate this particular labyrinth.

Church buildings can be tremendous resources to build relationships with people from the religions. Evangelicals differ as to whether their buildings are sacred spaces or not. The commonest view is that they are sacred by association with the Christian activities that go on in them. This puts some limits on the activities that can be held in them. Anglican churches are also seen as places where rites of civic religion are held. This could lead to requests by local government to hold inter-faith services based on a pluralist theology. Evangelicals cannot in good conscience be involved in such civic services.

# CHAPTER 5
# Dialogue

The emphasis on friendship as fundamental to witness in chapter 3 implies dialogue in the sense of conversation with people of the religions. 'Conversation' is a synonym of 'dialogue'. What was said about reaching adherents of the religions with the gospel emphasised that 'conversation' was foundational. It is in talking with them and listening to them in the context of our everyday living that we are able to share what is most precious to us as Christians – our knowledge of God through our Lord Jesus Christ. It is undoubtedly the case that most Christian witnessing is done in the context of ordinary conversation or dialogue.

But 'dialogue' is also defined in a more formal way as "discussion between representatives of two groups".[1] This chapter will consider evangelical Christian dialogue with adherents of the religions in this more formal sense. We shall consider first the presupposition with which we enter any dialogue and then look at a number of different types of dialogue in which evangelical Christians are engaged.

As evangelicals we reject categorically the theological/philosophical pluralist concept of dialogue. As stated in the previous

1   The Concise Oxford Dictionary

chapter theological/philosophical pluralists believe that the reality at the root of all the religions is one. So, for the pluralist the purpose of dialogue is for representatives from different religions to discover together the one ultimate reality that is at the root of their different traditions. Evangelical Christians cannot possibly share this presupposition when entering any dialogue with adherents of the religions.

Our presupposition is that God having spoken in many different ways through the prophets has spoken finally in His Son, the Lord Jesus Christ. Jesus as the way, the truth and the life has fully revealed the creator God and Father to humanity. Whatever dialogue we enter into we must enter with the presupposition of the supremacy of our Lord Jesus. This is not an arrogant claim. To claim that Jesus is supreme is not a claim to superiority but recognition of the amazing grace of God. Our deepest longing in any dialogue, therefore, must be that our dialogue partner should experience the same grace and come to know Jesus as their Saviour.

But even if our presupposition is the exclusive claims of Jesus, dialogue is not simply an opportunity for proclamation. Dialogue is not only an opportunity for us to make our convictions known but for us to hear the convictions of our dialogue partner(s). To dialogue we must meet face to face and with mutual respect listen to each other. It is as we do this that we will be able to understand each other, witness to each other – and in certain contexts trust each other enough to work together on matters of common interest.

We need to enter every dialogue as witnesses to the glory of Jesus. Our ultimate aim should always be that our dialogue partner(s) should see the glory of Jesus Christ and bow the knee to him. However, there are good intermediate aims as well that determine the type of dialogue in which we are engaged. We shall consider three different types of dialogue that differ because of their intermediate aims:

1 Apologetic/polemic

2 Scriptural reasoning

3 Fostering social cohesion and community understanding

# 1. Apologetic/polemic

Jesus wept over Jerusalem as he entered the city in triumph. He wept because of the blindness of the temple authorities and the teachers of the law. He wept because their blindness would ultimately cause untold misery to the ordinary people of the city. So, when we read the accounts of his dialogues with various representatives of the ruling classes and his withering condemnation of them we must not forget his tears. Everything our Lord did flowed from his heart of compassion. We can follow him in contending vigorously for the faith as long as our hearts are full of compassion.

Dialogue was deeply embedded in the culture of the Roman world into which the Church was born. The Greek method of philosophical teaching by means of question and answer had been spread widely throughout the empire by travelling philosophers. We see its influence even in Paul's letters where new sections begin with a question that gives Paul an opportunity to correct what is wrong in the question and then go on to persuade the imaginary questioner of the right way to think and act.[2] From reading his letters one can imagine how Paul argued

---

2 E.g. Romans 3:1ff; 6:1ff

"persuasively about the kingdom of God" in the synagogue in Ephesus (Acts 19:8) by means of dialogue and question and answer. And when he gave up on the synagogue and was either given or rented the lecture hall of Tyrannus he continued his discussions there on a daily basis. The lecture hall became a philosophical school of Jesus Christ and the dialogues/discussions held there, to which the Gentiles and Jews could easily relate, went on for two years and were a means to take the gospel way beyond Ephesus.

In Acts the most vigorous discussions were had with Jewish opponents of the gospel. Members of the Synagogue of the Freedmen, to which diaspora Jews from Cyrene, Alexandria, Cilicia and Asia belonged, argued with Stephen (Acts 6:9). The church in Achaia (Corinth) was encouraged when Apollos, who was an Alexandrian academic convert to the Way, arrived and "vigorously refuted the Jews in public debate, proving from the scriptures that Jesus was the Christ" (Acts 18:28).

Reasoned defence, otherwise known as 'apologetic', and controversial discussion (polemic) was undoubtedly a facet of the witness of the early Church. The cultural context was very conducive to this approach. Our cultural context may not be so conducive but where reasoned argument against our Christian faith is used we are justified in seeking opportunities for dialogue/discussion where we are given the opportunity to refute such arguments.

In engaging in dialogue or discussion it is vitally important to remember that the battle for the mind of our dialogue partner is a spiritual battle. Those that opposed Stephen "could not stand up against his wisdom or the Spirit by whom he spoke" (Acts 6:10). There were members of the church in Corinth that were undermining Paul and his message. Paul warns his opponents that he would not contend with them simply with weapons of worldly rhetoric but with the weapons of "divine power to demolish strongholds. We demolish arguments," he says, "and every pretension that sets itself up against the knowledge of God, and we take captive every thought to make it obedient to Christ" (2 Corinthians 10:4-5). It would be foolish to enter into apologetic or polemic dialogue with someone from another religion without a thorough knowledge of the truth of the gospel and of the beliefs of our dialogue partner(s). But it would be even more foolish to enter into such dialogue without the anointing of the Holy Spirit.

## Case studies

### Jay Smith[3]

He believes that the growing influence of radical Islam that has led to terrorist attacks such as 9/11 and 7/7 needs to be confronted with reasoned argument. Radical Islam is propagated on the basis of claims to the reliability of the Qur'an as a revelation from God and the superiority of Muhammad as a prophet from God. The Qur'an and Muhammad are claimed to be superior to the unreliable New Testament and Jesus, who is falsely claimed to be the Son of God. This radical Muslim movement has also seriously taken hold of the digital media so that many thousands of videos are available extoling the virtues of the Islamic foundations and attacking the foundations of Christianity.

---

3    What I've written here is based on his chapter *The Case for Polemics* in S. Bell and C. Chapman, *Between Naivety and Hostility*, Milton Keynes: Authentic, 2011, pp. 235-247 and watching some of his debates online. For written and video sources see http://www.debate.org.uk

While the Western response to this movement is repression and military force Jay believes that Christians should respond with reasoned argument. He has engaged in many recorded public debates with radical Muslim leaders that are freely available on the web. He and his team also regularly hold debates with Muslims at Hyde Park Corner in London.

Some significant Muslim leaders have become disciples of Jesus as a result and have become effective apologists in their own communities. Jay sees this as crucial to the future of Christian witness among Muslims.

**Imtiaz Khan, Ley Street Centre, London City Mission**
Imtiaz is a missionary with the London City Mission in Ilford, East London. This is how he describes the discussions that he has arranged with Muslims. The background to the discussions that he runs is a lot of bridge-building work with the Muslim community from the Ley Street Centre:

Many people believe it's impossible to hold meetings in which Christians and Muslims can ask each other open questions about their respective religions. They suspect that, if we ask each other tough questions, relationships will be damaged.

- Some choose not to speak.
- Some choose 'dialogue' - holding meetings in which Christians and Muslims can speak on specific topics to inform one another but never aim to refute each other's position.
- Other Christians instead choose 'debate' where arguments are presented in persuasive ways - refuting your opponent's opinions in order to prove a point. Keeping good relationships here takes second place to winning the day.

There are strengths and weakness to both dialogue and debate. Entering in to debate in order to win might encourage people to think but if it is done in a provocative and aggressive way it can have a negative impact. Engaging in dialogue without any challenge may build good friendships but rarely results in people changing their positions. So is there a different way that can keep balance?

Christian-Muslim discussions offer a helpful path between debate and dialogue.

Take the topic of "loving your neighbour": a dialogue would simply allow Christians and Muslims to share their respective beliefs on loving their neighbours. The Christian position could be presented by reflecting on the fact that Jesus taught that the whole law can be summed up in one command: "Love the Lord your God with all your heart, with all your soul and with all your mind … love your neighbour as yourself" (Matthew 22:37-39). Christians could go on to explain that Jesus defined "neighbour" by giving us the parable of The Good Samaritan. Muslims too could reflect on Muhammad's commands to treat your neighbours well. Listeners would end up learning that both Christianity and Islam teach people to love their neighbour.

A debate could cover much the same ground but with the aim of one side showing that they love their neighbours *better* than the other.

Christian-Muslim discussions, however, encourage those present to look, gently, at what makes each faith different. They tease out the fact that the Christian call to love is unique – because it is only in the Bible that the call to love those who are different, even those who are our enemies, rings out clearly.

There is a widespread perception among Muslims in Britain that Christianity is a man-made religion that cannot be proved true when scrutinised. At Ley Street Centre (LSC, one of London City Mission's centres) we hold 'Christian Muslim Discussions' (CMDs) once a month. We invite our Muslim friends to CMD meetings to compare and contrast Christianity and Islam. Some come eager to learn while others come keen to show that Christianity is nothing more than a fabrication. All are welcome. We love to clarify their misunderstandings about Christianity.

In these meetings we have seen that it is possible to maintain good relationships with our Muslim friends and, at the same time, be open and honest with each other. Christianity and Islam are compared and contrasted –respectfully and analytically.

We have discussed tough topics, such as "Who are the authors of the gospels?" "Can the gospels be trusted?" "Is there an evolution of Christology in the New Testament?" The reason we choose those topics is to convey the message that Christianity can be examined and scrutinised and yet still be proved true. Many Muslims read material online written by liberal and critical Christian scholars that undermines the message of Christianity and its credibility. Some Muslim friends use such material to justify their position. They may not choose to read what evangelical Christian scholars have written. So, at LSC we aim to present evangelical scholars' responses to common objections. If we do not address the issues and objections that Muslims and other critical scholars are raising, they will remain convinced that Christianity is untrue.

But alongside this, we give our Muslim friends the chance to speak to their own religion. We pose questions such as "Is the Qur'an God's final revelation?" "Who is the author of the Qur'an?" "Which is true: the Christian view of Jesus or the Islamic view of Jesus?" These topics can be considered quite provocative for some people but many Muslims are happy to talk about these things and love to engage with us rationally.

We need to realise what sort of questions Muslims are asking about Christianity here in Britain; and we should be open to discuss them. Many people judge Christianity purely on the basis of their experience of it (positive or negative). We need to look at it objectively and test the claims that Christianity is making. We should be happy to know that Christianity is a reasonable faith with evidence that can substantiate and verify its claims.

So let's be training people in apologetics so they can answer the questions that non-Christians are raising confidently, convincingly, boldly, effectively and biblically (I Peter 3:15). In short - let's enter into true Christian-Muslim discussion – whether that's on a large scale or in individual conversations.

And as we meet those many Muslims who come with great conviction that Islam is the truth – let's ask some rational questions of each other's religion without ever straying into the realms of being disrespectful. And as we do so, the truth of the cross shines out.

### Virtual dialogue
Inter-religious dialogue on the internet can create a virtual meeting place to enhance mutual understanding but it can also provide a place of witness that could be difficult to access in any other way. Of course adherents of the religions can and do use the internet extensively to witness to their faith. This should be an inspiration to evangelicals. Ali El-shariff Abdallah

Emmanuel witnesses to the effectiveness of dialogue on the internet. [4]

Family Life Network (now Squareone World Media), created various chat rooms for dialogue with Muslims. There was an 'Islamic Only Room' where searching questions were raised that would be difficult to raise in face-to-face meetings. From this room there were 'Private Rooms' that those who wanted to discuss the issues could enter and chat. There were also 'Rooms for Theological Challenges' in which doctrinal differences between Muslims and Christians could be discussed. Finally there were 'Christian Rooms for Witness' where the dialogue was exclusively about the Bible and Jesus Christ and the emphasis was on personal testimony and witness. The result of this work on the internet was 'hundreds of Muslim people coming to accept Jesus Christ as Lord and Saviour every month.[5]

## 2. Scriptural reasoning

This form of dialogue is associated in the UK with David Ford who is Regius Professor of Divinity and director of the Cambridge Inter-Faith Programme at the University of Cambridge. It was developed as a result of dissatisfaction with the pluralist view of dialogue on the one hand and the need for dialogue

-------

4    At the time of writing Emmanuel was associated with a broadcasting agency in Winnipeg called Family Life Network that had been known as Mennonite Brethren Communications from 1976-2000. The organisation that expanded its work into the digital world is now known as Squareone World Media. Arabic is one of the six languages in which it operates.

5    Ali El-shariff Abdallah Emmanuel 'The Internet and Dialogue Boxes' in J. R. Krabill, D. W. Shenk and L. Stutzman, eds, *Anabaptists Meeting Muslims: A Calling for Presence in the Way of Christ*, Scottdale: Herald Press, 2005, pp. 339-346

on the other because of the increasing tensions between the 'Christian' and 'Muslim' worlds. Because Israel is at the heart of the Christian-Muslim tension it is seen as vital to include Jews in the dialogue as well.

This type of dialogue has been developed between Christians, Muslims and Jews because it presupposes a belief in a revealed scripture as the fundamental authority in each of the religions. The way the dialogue is conducted is for representatives of the religions to bring texts on an agreed topic to share with each other. As this is done the differences between the traditions inevitably emerge but in such a way as to breed respect and mutual understanding – and often a deeper understanding of their own tradition by the presenters.

When asked in an interview about engaging in dialogue in order to find common ground this is how David Ford responded:

*"… in our experience, if you start off by seeking common ground, you tend to get a lowest common denominator from each of the traditions. You abstract something fairly thin that's not absolutely central to them, and you say, 'This is where we can come together.' And then at the first sign of trouble, there's an earthquake and the common ground dissolves. Now what we say as an alternative to seeking common ground in that form is to go deeply into the particular traditions of each, and try to find there ways of reaching towards things that have analogies in each tradition. In other words, that are similarities without being identities. You don't claim identity, because these traditions are obviously so deeply different in the way in which they have developed and are practised in the world today. But if you*

*engage with the scriptures, you make sure that you're on very different texts, that in relation to those texts you can never forget how different you are. And of course that can be more so in relation to Jews and Christians who share a common text. If you look at the different ways they interpret that text, then you see how deep the differences are there.*[6]

Although this type of dialogue was developed for Christians, Muslims and Jews because of their view of revelation there is no reason why it cannot be extended to other religions. For example, though Hindus and Buddhists have a very different view of revelation they still have sacred texts that deal with topics that are also dealt with in the Bible. Examples would be the understanding of the origin of the earth and human beings in the Hindu Rig Veda, the Hindu concept of incarnation (avatar) in the Bhagavad Gita or the Buddhist concept of the vicarious grace of the Bodhisattvas in the Saddharmapundarika Sutra.

This type of dialogue emerged in an academic setting and demands a high level of knowledge of religious texts. Its main value is in undermining theological pluralism and in fostering understanding between leaders in the various religions. The evangelical-inspired Centre for Muslim-Christian Studies in Oxford uses this approach. [7]

# 3. Community understanding – building friendship

We have already emphasised that friendship between Christians and adherents of the religions is crucial to our witness

---

6   http://www.pbs.org/wnet/religionandethics/2007/10/12/
    october-12-2007-interview-david-ford/4433/

7   http://cmcsoxford.org.uk

as evangelicals. We shall look at two examples where creating opportunities for dialogue is leading to friendship and co-operation in improving communities.

In those areas where there is a concentration of adherents of the religions there is clearly a need to build relationships on a community level. This will involve representatives from the different religions meeting together to improve their understanding of each other and to share their concerns for the place where they live together and its people. Responding to the data of the 2001 Census, social disturbances in 2001 and the events of 9/11 and 7/7, the Church of England has given much thought to the role of the Church, especially in areas that have a high concentration of adherents of the religions. This has led to forming a movement called Presence and Engagement. This is a movement for the whole Church of England that has four main centres in London, Birmingham, Leicester and Bradford.

## A Hindu-Christian dialogue: misunderstandings about evangelism

When the Archbishop of Canterbury stated (in 2013) that one of his priorities was evangelism, some Hindus wondered what lay behind this. Was it an indication that they would be targeted? There was a lot of suspicion that Christians were out to 'convert', with aggressive methods. A small group of Hindus and Christians from the UK's Hindu Christian Forum met with some of the Archbishop's advisers to explore this further.

Examples were given of how Christians have sometimes lacked integrity in their methods, attracting people with social care, manipulating them with emotional inducements or using the power of money. Many of the examples were from India, though some were from the UK as well. Behind these lay historical memories of the colonial past: "When you say that Jesus is the only way, doesn't that mean a feeling of superiority?"

The Christians acknowledged mistakes and, sometimes, wrong methods. A turning point in the conversation came when it was explained that evangelism is 'sharing good news about Jesus' and is not about inducing or forcing people to change their religion. Attitudes changed and the discussion went deeper in asking questions and sharing personal perspectives more openly. For example, there was a very real concern over the tendency of some who are converted to react by "hating, fearing or degrading the Hindu heritage". And on the other side there could be a tendency to suspect conspiracy or question motives. The same activity – caring for the sick – can be interpreted in very different ways. One says: "We do it because we love them and at the same time we tell them about Jesus' love for them." Another says: "Your real agenda is conversion and the rest is simply a cover".

As a result of this discussion it was agreed that we need to demythologise and clear misunderstanding. Work had already begun on ethical guidelines in this area of conversion and it was agreed this should continue.

A Hindu member of the group concluded:

> "We managed to have a very open and honest conversation and felt that there is enough trust and honesty in our relationship that we should have a second meeting – I suggested it should be at my house as it is time that we become friends. We are going to be accused of all kinds of things but must have faith in each other to walk together to bring better understanding and avoid easily misunderstood actions."

In the face of persistent misunderstandings which can make the 'good news' sound like bad news, this kind of discussion builds trust and respect.

**St Philip's Centre, Leicester**
The work of this centre is described in *Sharing the Gospel of Salvation*, which was a report presented to the General Synod of the Church of England in 2010. While the work of the centre is far broader than 'dialogue', dialogue in its broader sense of meeting, developing mutual understanding, serving together for the common good and providing the context for authentic witness, is fundamental to its existence:

Leicester developed as a city with significant communities of other faiths primarily from the early 1970s with the expulsion of Asians from Uganda under General Idi Amin. From that time have grown substantial Hindu and Sikh and also Muslim communities, including latterly a significant Somali population. The city authorities suggest figures of 41 per cent non-indigenous population, and 52 per cent in the schools (of a population just fewer than 300,000). Estimates are that Hindus and Muslims are about equal in number, and there is a significant move of more prosperous South Asians to suburban and rural Leicestershire.

St Philip's parish has been among many parishes that have changed dramatically in recent decades. From being a substantial congregation drawing on a parish population of Christian culture, the church has moved to being a small congregation in a parish with the 8th smallest Christian percentage population in the UK and set in the midst of Muslim, Hindu and Sikh people. The church building now faces a substantial newly built mosque across the road, a miniature version of one of the great domed mosques in Istanbul, with several hundred attending each day, and with no places available on Fridays or during Ramadan.

Two crucial decisions were made in relationship to the church. A major fire in 1996 led to debate as to whether to remain open, in view of the changing demography around. The bishop of the time took the decision that for this very reason they should remain open as a living witness, and a major refurbishment took place to allow for community use. The second decision was made in 2005 to remain present and to engage with this changed context in a strikingly new way and the St. Philip's Centre for Study and Engagement in a Multi-Faith Society has developed from this decision.

The Parochial Church Council decided to enter into a partnership with the Diocese of Leicester and the national Presence and Engagement programme to become a means through which the experience of living out the gospel in the midst of people of other faiths could be offered to other churches locally and regionally. To this end it invested part of its financial reserves, its vicarage, its church buildings and its lived life in the creation and sustaining of the St Philip's Centre.

St Philip's Centre is rooted in the multi-faith context of Leicester and is a national ecumenical training centre under the Presence and Engagement initiative. It provides training for Christians, for those of other faiths and for civic partners. It enables Christians and churches to be a confident presence in a multi-faith world, prepared to share their own faith and learn from others. Good working relationships and dialogue with peoples of other faiths serve to promote the common good.

From its experience of engagement with congregations, other faiths and public sector authorities, a range of programmes and opportunities have been developed, including for example:

- **Unfamiliar Journey** – an ecumenical course for people who are interested in encouraging Christian witness and building good relations with people of different faiths.
- **Presence and Engagement in a Multi-Faith Society** – a three-day course for clergy and experienced lay people of all denominations.
- **A course for chaplaincy and pastoral care** in a multi-faith society.
- **MA in Inter-religious Relations,** accredited by the De Montfort University.
- **Senior leadership training workshops**.

Alongside these professional training courses, the centre also hosts a range of forums: a 'Family of Abraham' group made up of people in mixed faith marriages; two Muslim Christian dialogue groups, one for women only; a Sikh-Christian forum and a Hindu-Christian Forum. Many of these have met regularly for over six years. Wider outreaching activities include high profile sporting events including annual football and cricket matches between Imams and Christian clergy both locally and inter-regionally which spread a Christian message of harmony and the enjoyment of life together. It is a key partner with the Leicester Council of Faiths (now 23 years in existence), the Faith Leaders' Forum convened by the bishop, and facilitated by the director and bishop's chaplain since 2001, and the newly-formed Leicestershire Faiths Forum.

St Philip's has a collaborative relationship with the Islamic Foundation's educational centre at Markfield in the training of Muslim chaplains to work in hospitals, prisons and higher education.

As a direct result of the centre's dynamism, the whole Christian congregation of St Philip's church has flourished, sharing in and contributing to the sense of energy, achievement and shared purpose of the centre. There were more than 43 events in the church building over 2009, its centenary year, which is now seen as the centre of a small but thriving Christian community rather than a partially disused building. The congregation has grown to include young children and people from different ethnic backgrounds.

What might be the learning to be drawn from this experience and to be shared with others?

- That continuous physical presence in a community whose nature is radically changing provides the basis for deep engagement with incoming people of other faiths.

- That a shared and mutually supportive relationship between the local church, the diocese and other Christian denominations brings benefits of resources, encouragement and common purpose. Core support from the bishop, the Bishop's Council and the Diocesan Synod, has been vital, and generous, as the centre is seen as a centre for mission.

- That an explicitly Christian community can be appreciated, respected and used by other faith communities and by secular authorities in a wide range of programmes for the common good.

- That a strong local centre can contribute greatly to the international, national and regional Church and beyond, through the wide use of its staff, several of whom have an academic reputation, and especially are known for their linking of the academic with the practical.

- That multi-faith relations are about relations also with

particular faith communities. Leicester and the centre provide an ideal base for engaging with 'Indic' faiths, in balance with Islam and Judaism.

- That a centre can be deeply rooted in Christ, and in Christian scripture, clear about the saving grace of God offered in Christ, but at the same time, be deeply committed to the message that "There's a wideness in God's mercy."[8]

**The Feast**

This is a movement to create dialogue between Christian and Muslim young people birthed within Scripture Union through the inspiration of Andrew Smith. It became an independent charity as The Feast in 2008. This is the website description of what it does:

*"At the heart of The Feast is a desire to bring together teenagers of different faiths to build friendships, explore faith and change lives."*

The way we work is to build good relationships with groups of Christian and Muslim young people and then invite them to 'encounter' events where they can meet one another. The relationships with the young people have to be developed in distinctive ways, as their varied communities have different structures and youth programmes based on faith and culture.

Our events are totally youth focused. A typical event involves warm-up activities, discussion starters, group work, games and refreshments. We adopt good youth work practice and have the interests and needs of the young people at heart. Over

8    pp. 22-24. The report can be accessed via http://presenceandengagement.org.uk/sharing-gospel-salvation

the years we have found that small events (typically 20 young people maximum) have a much greater impact on the young people than large events, and we work hard to make sure there are equal numbers of each participating faith group.

**Exploring faith** At each 'encounter' event, after breaking the ice, we set up the ground rules for their time together, called our *Guidelines for Dialogue*. This creates a safe space where the young people are willing to share their own honest thoughts and feelings. As a result we can then facilitate open discussions between the young people, based on them speaking about their own faith and so learning about the similarities and differences that exist. We believe that acknowledging both similarities and differences is vital if we are to be honest about our faiths and be equipped to deal with disagreements when they arrive.

The topics we discuss are ones of concern to young people rather than ones that faith leaders, theologians or other adults think they ought to be discussing. Through this we enable the young people to share their beliefs, experiences and ideas with one another rather than telling them what they ought to be sharing.

**Creating friendships** These personal faith conversations, based on mutual vulnerability and respect, are an excellent environment for forming new friendships. Young people are helped to overcome the fears and gain the confidence to live well with people who are from a different community or faith, and can sit together, enjoy food, laughs and honest and open conversations.

**Changing lives** We encourage young people to take the lessons from The Feast out into their everyday lives. This may mean confronting their own prejudices and seeking to make positive changes in their own lives, families and communities. This may also lead to young people leading on social action initiatives like litter picks, collecting food for and visiting needy people, and proactive peaceful protest against injustice. We are proud to see this diverse group of young people making such positive change in their families, schools, neighbourhoods and communities, and maybe the world.

Some adults – Christian and Muslim - express unease at encouraging young people to befriend Muslims/Christians in a context that positively encourages the young people to share their faith from fear that they may convert. From the Christian perspective there is little evidence of exposure leading to conversion to Islam. The conversion that Christian young people make on a massive scale is to the prevailing secular consumerist idolatry. Being friends with Muslims could even help Christian young people resist the temptation to go the same way as their peers because they are also resisting the same temptation.[9]

## Conclusion

While it is now very widely accepted among evangelicals that conversation with those that are not followers of Jesus is fundamental to evangelism, the focus of this chapter is on creating more formal situations where dialogue can happen.

--------------------------------------------------------------

9    Andrew Smith has written extensively about this type of dialogue among young people. For a summary see *Working with Muslim and Christian Young People* in S.Bell and C Chapman, *Between Naivety and Hostility; uncovering the best Christian responses to Islam in Britain*, Authentic: Milton Keynes, 2011, pp. 203-217. See also *Faith, Friendship and Pedagogy: Equipping Christian teenagers for a relevant engagement with Muslim peers*, TH.D. theses, Uni. Of Birmingham, 2007, which is available for downloading from the British Library.

While emphasising the need to listen and respect those from the religions with whom we dialogue we reject the theological/philosophical pluralist approach that the purpose of dialogue is to discover the one ultimate reality that is the essence of all religions. For the evangelical, the value of any form of dialogue is judged by its ability to create a context for authentic witness.

Where possible it can be right to defend our faith in the face of charges made against it, (apologetic), and point out the weaknesses of another religion (polemic) – with the assumption that our dialogue partner will reciprocate. There are crucial qualifications needed before venturing into apologetic and polemic dialogue – a thorough knowledge, the ability to argue clearly and a heart full of love and grace.

It is also possible that more can be done to tap into the potential of the web to engage in apologetic and polemic dialogue.

There is scope at the more academic level to engage in dialogue that is more focused on mutual understanding. Scriptural reasoning is one method that has been developed to achieve this end. Where scriptural texts are exegeted and expounded with faith in the Bible as God's word scriptural reasoning is clearly a context for authentic witness, as well as a means of building understanding.

Dialogue to build community understanding has been developed to overcome segregation in society – where religious and non-religious communities live in the same place but have hardly any contact. In this case dialogue may not focus on religion specifically but on how the religious and non-religious can co-operate together to improve the quality of life where they live. This type of dialogue is to be welcomed not only as a means of breaking down barriers and building social cohesion but also as a means of opening the door to authentic witness.

**To become the context for authentic witness, all the various types of dialogue need strong faith and devotion to Jesus, a strong sense of the Spirit's presence and a deep commitment to prayer.**

# CHAPTER 6

# Education

## The 'Trojan Horse' letter

The 1983 Evangelical Alliance report discussed many issues that are still relevant when thinking about the role of religion in education. In the state-funded sector the role of Christian teachers and the issue of school assemblies is still relevant. In the private sector the nature and merits of a Christian education is still debated.

But there has been a big change in what is happening on the ground, especially in some inner city areas. In November 2013 Birmingham City Council received a copy of what has become known as the 'Trojan Horse' letter. The subsequent enquiry into what was apparently evidence of an attempt by a Muslim group to propagate a method for influencing education in their interest raised fundamental questions about the role of religion in state-funded education.

The appointment of Peter Clarke by the Department for Education to act as an education commissioner to look into the claims made in the 'Trojan Horse' letter was controversial but his report was generally considered to be a fair and objective assessment of the considerable body of evidence that was gathered. His firm conclusion was that "there has been a determined effort to gain control of governing bodies at a small number of schools by people who are associated with each other. Once in a position to do so, they have sought to introduce a distinct set of Islamic behaviours and religious practices".[1]

He also considered whether those that were seeking to influence their schools were representing their Muslim community as a whole. His conclusion was that they did not but actually represented a particular ideology within Islam that disparaged other Muslim groups as well as the West in general. His main evidence for this was the posts of a Facebook group called the 'Park View Brotherhood'. The group was set up and administered by the acting principal of Park View School and its members were influential male teachers in the school.

This is how Clarke describes what he found in the posts of this Facebook group:

> "There is ample evidence that individuals who hold or have held key positions in the schools have a shared ideological basis to their faith. During the investigation I took possession of the contents of a social media discussion between a group of teachers at Park View School that for much of 2013 was called the 'Park View Brotherhood'. It was initiated and administered by Mr Monzoor Hussain, the Acting Principal, and was joined by influential teachers within the school. The evidence from more than 3,000 messages spread over 130 pages of transcript shows that this group either promoted or failed to challenge views that are grossly

1   Peter Clarke, 'Report into allegations concerning Birmingham schools arising from the 'Trojan Horse' letter, https://www.gov.uk/government/publications/birmingham-schools-education-commissioners-report', p.10

*intolerant of beliefs and practices other than their own. The all-male group discussions include explicit homophobia; highly offensive comments about British service personnel; a stated ambition to increase segregation in the school; disparagement of strands of Islam; scepticism about the truth of reports of the murder of Lee Rigby and the Boston bombings; and a constant undercurrent of anti-Western, anti-American and anti-Israeli sentiment. Some postings were challenged by the administrator, Mr Hussain, but generally only where criticism was made of other Muslim groups. The numerous endorsements of hyperlinks to extremist speakers betray a collective mind-set that can fairly be described as an intolerant Islamist approach that denies the validity of alternative beliefs, lifestyles and value systems, including within Islam itself."[2]*

Issues such as how to respond to extremist religious views will be considered in the chapter on politics. What concerns us here is the attempt to use a state-funded education system to promote one particular religious view – in this case an Islamist view. The 'Trojan Horse' enquiry showed that there are legally possible ways of dominating a governing body of a state-funded school. Once in place such a dominating group can bring pressure to bear to remove an unsympathetic head teacher and appoint a head teacher sympathetic to their cause. The 'Trojan Horse' letter claimed that such groups could further the cause of their religious emphasis within the state school sector.

---

2    Ibid. p. 11

# State-funded schools with a religious character[3]

The irony of the situation is that there is a perfectly legal and legitimate route for religious groups to be state-funded because around a third of all schools in England and Wales are state-funded schools with a religious character. Over 20 per cent of all schools are Church of England and around 10 per cent Roman Catholic. In 2010 there were one Hindu, 38 Jewish, 11 Muslim and four Sikh state-funded schools. The non-Christian state funded schools with a religious character together represent less than one per cent of all state-funded schools. The overwhelming majority of state-funded schools with a religious character are either Church of England or Roman Catholic. In Scotland and Northern Ireland almost all the schools with a religious character are Roman Catholic. In Scotland 14 per cent are schools with a religious character – all Roman Catholic except three Episcopalian and one Jewish. It is difficult to find the percentage of schools with a religious character in Northern Ireland but in 2012 around 50 per cent of primary pupils were in Roman Catholic schools with a religious character.

## *Historical background*

The fact that such a large proportion of state-funded schools in the UK are schools with a religious character is a legacy of the time when education was seen as the responsibility of the state church. Up to the late 17<sup>th</sup> century in England and Wales the Church of England had almost total control of education. By the beginning of the 19<sup>th</sup> century with the growth of

---

3   This is the technically correct term for what are generally called 'faith schools'. The Church of England are adamant that they do not run 'faith schools'.

non-conformist churches that also saw education as a priority the situation was radically changed. This was especially the case when the churches sought to provide education for the poor as the population exploded in the 19th century.

Within the Church of England the National Society[4] was formed and became the largest provider of education for the poor. The National Society schools were specifically meant to make good Anglicans of the pupils as well as give them a basic education. The non-conformist churches established the much smaller British Society. These schools taught the basic principles of the Protestant Christian faith without the peculiarities of any one denomination.

By the middle of the 19th century the inability of the churches to provide even a basic education for all children led to state intervention. This began by the state supporting the National and British school societies with grants. When this proved inadequate and it became clear that the state was going to have to provide the bulk of the funding for universal primary education the issue of who controlled what happened in the schools inevitably arose. In 1872 the Church of Scotland handed over its schools to the state. Because of its size and power the Church of England was able to keep considerable control of its schools even though they became state-funded schools. With the growth of the Roman Catholic Church on the UK mainland in the 19th century, due to Irish immigration in particular, the re-instated Roman Catholic hierarchy was also able to negotiate a similar pattern of state funding for their schools.

----

4    The full name of the society was National Society for the Promotion of the Education of the Poor in the Principles of the Established Church. It was established in 1811 and continues to operate having celebrated its 200th anniversary in 2011.

The definitive incorporation of church schools into the state-funded education system happened as a result of the 1944 Education Act. There have been a number of significant education acts since 1944 but the agreement made between Church and state in that act has remained substantially in force.

Particularly in England the 1944 Act gave birth to a dual system of state-funded education – schools with a religious character and schools without a religious character. There are two main types of state funded schools with a religious character. Most of them (59 per cent) are voluntary-aided – including almost all the Roman Catholic, Jewish, Muslim and Sikh schools. The governing body in these schools control admissions policy and if oversubscribed the school can have 100 per cent of its pupils from one faith. The governing body also has the right to appoint teachers and supplementary staff that are adherents of the school's faith. Pupils in voluntary-aided faith schools are obliged to follow the national curriculum but religious education can be taught in accordance with the schools' religious affiliation unless parents request otherwise. Local authorities pay all the running costs of voluntary-aided schools and have an obligation to pay 90 per cent of capital costs while the buildings are held in trust by the faith group that gives its name to the school.

Most of the rest (36 per cent) are voluntary-controlled including the majority of Church of England schools.[5] They apply the admissions policy of the local authority, although some authorities allow them to operate in the same way as voluntary-aided schools and apply a faith test to their pupils. They can apply a

5   The remaining five per cent are foundation schools, free schools or academies.

faith test to only 20 per cent of their teaching staff, are funded completely by local authorities and must follow the national curriculum and also the state-approved curriculum for religious education.

Interestingly, though the non-conformists ceded control of their schools to the state, the state substantially adopted their approach to the role of religion in education in the 1944 Act. Religious education became compulsory in all state schools and until the last quarter of the 20th century this meant that pupils were taught in outline the content of the Bible, particularly the New Testament, as understood by Christians. Added to this it became compulsory for state-funded schools to provide an act of Christian worship on a daily basis to all pupils. This act of worship was to be Christian but not denominational. A provision to opt out of RE lessons or the act of collective worship was put in place for adherents of religions other than Christian and for non-believers. Since 1944 other acts have ruled that religious education and the act of collective worship must reflect the increasing religious diversity in society while continuing to be primarily Christian.

## Current settlement

The movement to provide schools with a religious character shows no sign of waning. Since 2001 the number of places in Church of England primary schools has increased and 100 new church secondary schools have been established providing 54,000 school places. The popularity of faith schools is now being recognised by government proposals for expansion in the years ahead.

Many evangelicals believe that to have so many Christian schools with a religious character funded by the state is a blessing and an opportunity and that the focus should be on improving the Christian quality of such schools. In making the case for such schools it is maintained that parents of religions other than Christianity prefer to send their children to these schools because of the moral standards that they maintain. It is also claimed that while schools with a religious character provide education for adherents of a particular faith/religion church schools are open to everyone in the community where the school is placed. As Nigel Genders, the Church of England's chief education officer claims: "Our schools are not faith schools for Christians but church schools for all."[6]

However, it has to be admitted that the admissions policy of schools with a religious character has been subject to severe criticism.[7] The fact that Church of England schools have the right to prefer members of the Church of England does potentially lead to the abuse of parents attending church simply to get their children into a particular school. Nigel Genders' statement can be seen as an acknowledgment of the problems relating to admissions policy.

While affirming the openness of their schools the Church of England in recent reports has strongly re-affirmed the fact that their schools exist as a crucial aspect of the Church's mission to propagate the Christian faith. For example, *The Church School of the Future Review* states that "putting faith and spiritual development at the heart of the curriculum and ensuring

----

6   *Church Times*, May 1st 2015

7   The British Humanist Association published a report on behalf of the Fair Admissions Campaign in 2015 entitled *An Unholy Mess*. The report is available at http://fairadmissions.org.uk/wp-content/uploads/2015/09/An-Unholy-Mess.pdf

that a Christian ethos permeates the whole educational experience"[8] is central to its educational provision. To achieve this the report emphasises the continuing control of governing bodies by church representatives, the appointment of Christian head teachers, the teaching of religious education in which the teaching of Christianity predominates and regular Christian worship in school assemblies.

The report quoted in the last paragraph also referred to another report published in 2010 entitled *Going for Growth: Transformation for Children, young people and the church* that "set out a rationale and programme for Christian nurture of children and young people. It issued a call… for action based on three key premises that apply to children of the faith, of other faiths and of no faith". The first of these key premises was to "work towards every child and young person having a life-enhancing encounter with the Christian faith and the person of Jesus Christ".[9]

In the context of this reaffirmation of the missional nature of church schools work is being done on putting "faith and spiritual development at the heart of the curriculum". A good example of this is the Grove Booklet entitled *Distinctively Christian learning?* by Trevor and Margaret Cooling.[10] Their basic premise

8   See *The Church School of the Future Review*, Church of England Archbishop's Council Education Division/The National Society, 2012 p. 3

9   ibid. p. 9

10  *Grove Education: Distinctively Christian Learning?*, Trevor and Margaret Cooling, Grove Books: Cambridge, 2013. 'What if learning' was developed by David Smith of the Kuyers Institute in the US.  His books include *Learning from the Stranger: Christian Faith and Cultural Diversity*, Wm. B. Eerdmans, 2009, David Smith and Barbara M. Carvill *The Gift of the Stranger: Faith, Hospitality, and Foreign Language Learning*, Wm. B. Eerdmans, 2000, and David Smith and James K. A. Smith, *Teaching and Christian Practices: Reshaping Faith and Learning*, Wm. B. Eerdmans, 2011.

is that Christianity has a "vision for humanity" that can and should be reflected in the whole curriculum. The method they advocate is called 'What If Learning'. [11] There are three steps in this method of developing a way of teaching that reflects the Christian vision of humanity. The implications of these steps for the way a subject is taught is illustrated from the teaching of a foreign language:

1) **Seeing anew** – reimagining a piece of work to reflect a distinctively Christian vision for humanity. In the case of teaching a foreign language this could mean moving "from viewing language learning as preparation for tourism to seeing it anew as a preparation for offering hospitality to strangers".

2. **Choosing engagement** – developing learning activities to reflect the new way of seeing. "In the foreign languages example this was the use of conversation activities that focused on relationships rather than transactions."

3. **Reshaping practice** – bringing classroom practice into line with the new vision. "In the foreign languages example this was the decision to use photos of real people rather than cartoons."[12]

Though aimed specifically at teachers in church schools there is no reason to inhibit Christian teachers using the method described in Trevor and Margaret Cooling's book in non-church schools. The deepest values that everyone has are rooted in worldviews that are underpinned by beliefs. This is as true for the humanist as it is for an ardent Hindu. There is no such thing

11  See www.whatiflearning.co.uk and www.transforminglives.org.uk for
    more information about this approach and its background

12  Trevor and Margaret Cooling op. cit. p. 9.

as a neutral value. A teacher using this method would simply be openly reflecting this reality and could challenge colleagues to look at the roots of the values that they inculcate through their teaching.[13]

## Schools with a religious character and social cohesion

At the moment the number of schools with a religious character affiliated to religions other than Christianity - the Church of England or the Roman Catholic Church - is very small but there is no legal reason to hinder the multiplication of such schools. Some evangelicals would consider such a development as undesirable believing that their proliferation would be a threat to social cohesion.[14] Studies of schools with a religious character other than Christian indicate a high percentage of pupils from non-white ethnic groups, which is suggestive that they are also from the same religion. However, the ethnic profile of pupils in non-religious schools in areas where there is a high density of people of Asian origin is similar to that of Sikh or Muslim schools with a religious character. Schools with or without a religious character in such areas do not reflect the UK-wide population.[15] The issue does not seem to be the reli-

----

13  See Trevor Cooling, *Doing God in Education*, Theos, 2010 available at http://www.theosthinktank.co.uk/publications/2010/12/02/doing-god-in-education

14  See the 2014 report by the Theos thinktank, *More than an Educated Guess: Assessing the evidence on faith schools* concludes 'that there is little reason to think that faith schools are socially divisive.' http://www.theosthinktank.co.uk/publications/2013/10/02/more-than-an-educated-guess-assessing-the-evidence-on-faith-schools p. 9.

15  See the Demos Integration Hub study on Education Section 2 'School segregation' at http://www.integrationhub.net/module/education/

gious or non-religious character of the schools but that white British parents choose not to send their children to schools where there is a majority of pupils from other, especially Asian, ethnic origin.

The fact that pupils of Asian origin in particular are increasingly being educated substantially in schools with a high level of segregation should concern us as evangelicals whether their schools are schools with a religious character or not. The establishing of more Muslim or Sikh schools could theoretically exacerbate the situation but the fundamental issue is segregation. What happened in Birmingham was not a consequence of religious schooling but of segregated schooling.

Those that oppose the establishment of schools with a religious character because they pose a threat to social cohesion often point to the example of Northern Ireland. In Northern Ireland, the situation is complex and systemic but schools are largely made up of a majority of either Protestant or Catholic children. In the main Protestant children go to state-controlled schools and Roman Catholic children tend to go to Roman Catholic schools that are grant-maintained by the Department for Education. So, most children grow up with hardly any contact, in school at least, with children of the 'other side' of the main social divide in Northern Ireland. Only five per cent of pupils go to integrated schools that, through their admissions criteria, ensure approximately equal numbers of Protestant and Catholic children. Separating children for their education may not be the main cause of social tension there but at the very least it has contributed to the perpetuation of division and conflict. It is much harder to befriend someone we have never met than someone we have sat in class and played with for years.[16]

In light of the experience of Northern Ireland many lessons could be learned when it comes to schools with a religious character. Some evangelicals believe that a moratorium on the establishment of state-funded schools with a religious character is essential for the preservation of social cohesion. Some even advocate the establishment of a fully secular system of state-funded education where no religion is privileged and where those who want a Christian, Hindu, Muslim etc education for their children would have to pay for the privilege.[17] To transition to such a system, which would be similar to the system in the US, would be traumatic since a third of UK schools are schools with a religious character. Such a transition is very unlikely in the short term at least. Meanwhile the problem of religious/ethnically segregated education as a simple reflection of demographic realities is intensifying and this is a situation that urgently needs to be addressed.

## The Christian teacher

School teaching is a noble Christian vocation. Teachers can be found in most evangelical churches and ought to be strongly supported as they seek to serve the Lord in what is often a very challenging situation. Evangelical churches are renowned for their support of 'missionaries' that have gone abroad to serve the Lord but often neglect to support the 'missionary' teachers seeking to reflect the glory of Jesus in their local schools.

---

16 See *Christianity and Other Faiths: An Evangelical Contribution to our Multi-faith Society*, Exeter: Paternoster, 1983, p. 44

17 The think tank Ekklesia is an example although many would argue that it has left its evangelical moorings. See http://www.ekklesia.co.uk

The qualities of a good Christian teacher as described in the www.transforminglives.co.uk website are relevant to all teachers including those that teach in schools with many adherents of religions other than Christianity:

Most Christian teachers regard the quality of their relationships with their pupils and colleagues as a key element in the difference they can make in schools. Their approach can be summed up in two ideas:

1.  Servant leadership - following Christ's example of leading by being the servant of others.

2.  Integrity - the most widespread criticism of Christians is that they are hypocrites. Being a person of integrity is very important. If you are known as a Christian, people will expect this of you.

This will show in a number of ways.
* Treating pupils with respect and trust

* Keeping promises

* Being fair and being just

* Wanting the best for pupils

* Being prepared to listen

* Providing support in times of difficulty

* Being involved in extra-curricular activities

* Celebrating pupils' successes

* Not holding grudges

* Not giving up on a difficult pupil

* Defending pupils against the system when necessary

* Working hard and doing a good job

None of this is the same as being 'matey' with pupils; you are not a youth worker. Rather it is about respecting your pupils and wanting to see each of them fulfil their God-given potential.[18]

# Religious education

The provision of religious education for all pupils is a statutory requirement in UK schools. Each authority is required to have an agreed syllabus for the subject having regard to the national framework provided for the subject provided by the Department for Education. Added to this "the Education Act 1996 states that an agreed syllabus must reflect the fact that the religious traditions in Great Britain are in the main Christian, while taking account of the teachings and practices of the other principal religions represented in Great Britain".[19] This means that "Christianity should be studied throughout each key stage" and other religions (Buddhism, Hinduism, Judaism, Islam and Sikhism) "across the key stages".[20] This means that parents and other interested parties have the right to expect that pupils will gain a good understanding of Christianity and some understanding of other religions while at school.

The framework also states that pupils ought to be free to share their religious convictions without fear of embarrassment or ridicule and that they should learn to appreciate the significance of interfaith dialogue that highlights the similarities and differences between religions.[21] In practice the prevailing

---

18  See http://www.transforminglives.org.uk/already-teaching/day-by-day/making-a-difference-in-school-life

19  http://www.legislation.gov.uk/ukpga/1996/56/part/V/chapter/III This is section 375 of the Act.

20  Ibid. p.12.

21  Ibid. p. 12-13.

pluralistic philosophy/theology of religious education and religious studies since the 1970s has militated against the tolerant approach advocated in the framework. If teachers have been trained to assume that religions are but different paths to the same reality they will go into teaching with a presumption that any pupil with a strong conviction that their religion is the true path to God is misguided and in need of being directed into the true pluralist understanding. One way of doing this is to focus on topics such as the problem of evil or the existence of God in philosophy of religion.

In an extensive study of the way in which pupils with strong religious convictions experience religious education, Daniel Moulin came to some significant conclusions that need to be seriously taken on board by RE teachers:

1  They complained about the way their religion was misrepresented.

2  RE was experienced as a 'difference blind liberalism' – its theological pluralist assumptions left no real space for authentic difference.

3  The way the philosophy of religion was taught made them feel that they were under attack.

4  RE did not protect pupils from the hostility of their secular peers. "Because of the hostility of their peers, and ignorance or bias of their teachers, the classroom was not always a safe place to be open about their religious identity."

5  Teachers often lacked the knowledge to be able to defend religious pupils when they were 'attacked' by their peers.[22]

---

22  The points are a brief summary of the conclusions of Daniel Moulin, RE Online Thinkpiece: 'What religious students have to tell us about RE', http://www.reonline.org.uk/news/thinkpiece-what-religious-students-have-to-tell-us-about-re-dr-daniel-moulin/

Church leaders and parents have a right to expect that RE will major on Christianity as well as provide a basic understanding of other major religious traditions. That we all need some understanding of religions other than Christianity is clearly essential in our multi-religious society. That Christianity should be given more attention is also defensible on the grounds that UK history and culture has been so shaped by Christianity that a thorough understanding of the faith is essential as a basis for understanding so much else that is taught in the school curriculum. Even in a secularised state school system it would be necessary to privilege the teaching of Christianity.

We also have a right to expect that the religious convictions of Christian pupils are fully respected and that the RE lesson is a safe place for them to express their faith without fear of bullying from the teacher or their peers. The research of Moulin and others suggest that it may be time for religious leaders and parents to alert schools to the reality of religious bullying.

## Religious assemblies

The section on religious assemblies in the 1983 Evangelical Alliance report concluded that: "Christians have some radical thinking to do in the area of school worship in the multi-faith school." The legal position has not changed since 1983. All schools in England, Wales and Northern Ireland are still obliged in law to provide an act of 'collective worship' for each child every day.[23] In Scotland they call it an act of 'religious observance' that is expected to promote the spiritual development of all pupils and celebrate the values of the school.

---

23 In Northern Ireland where the overwhelming majority of schools are either Protestant or Roman Catholic the collective act of worship is almost always Christian.

What was said in the 1983 Alliance report regarding keeping the law on religious assemblies, especially in schools that have a large proportion of pupils from non-Christian religions, is still relevant:

> "Clearly multi-faith acts of worship are impossible in school. The use of such basic terms as 'God' and 'prayer' have such different meanings in different religions that the activity becomes of little meaning, save to inculcate the equal validity of faiths. Schools faced with this predicament may present an act of Christian worship… and allow dissenters to withdraw. However, this is divisive for the school community and assumes a commitment to Christianity on the part of the majority – which may well be an erroneous assumption."[24]

The situation is further exasperated in schools with a majority of adherents of the religions that is now the reality in many inner city schools.

One of the major challenges that head teachers face in trying to fulfil the demands of the law on collective worship is finding teachers that are capable and willing to lead such an act because the number of teachers that are familiar with worship is diminishing. This has led to widespread ignoring of the law. But while the law is in place it provides an opportunity for Christian teachers, schools workers and church leaders to enable head teachers to keep the law. In this context the advice given to teachers in the Transforming Lives website is relevant for everyone who grasps this opportunity:

1 Focus on *sharing* your faith, not *imposing* your faith. This creates a very different feel for everyone attending.

---

24 *Christianity and Other Faiths: An Evangelical Contribution to our Multi-faith Society,* Exeter: Paternoster, 1983, p. 43

2 Remember that this gathering is compulsory, so don't do things that force pupils to participate in worship. For example don't say 'let us pray'; rather say something like: 'I am going to say a prayer which you can join in with if you want by saying Amen at the end'.

3 Ask yourself what you would feel comfortable with if you were in an assembly led by someone of a different faith from you. Then behave in the same way.

4 Always think about the pupils and their parents. Will they be comfortable with how you are leading?[25]

# Christian schools

The focus of the 1983 report was more on the inadequacies of the state system of education that was then dominated by a particular humanistic approach than on the repercussion for education of the growth of religions other than Christianity. The report felt that parents were justified in opting for Christian schools simply because the standards of education in the state system were so bad. Since then the performance of state schools has come under scrutiny and there is now a very heavy emphasis on improving their performance. In England this has led to the establishment of academies and free schools that are directly responsible to the secretary of state for education rather than to local government. Many of these schools are either church schools or have a strong Christian foundation.

In Wales schools remain under the control of local authorities but the emphasis on improving the performance of pupils in public examinations is as intense as it is in England. The drive to improve standards in mathematics and English (or Welsh

25 http://www.transforminglives.org.uk/already-teaching/day-by-day/making-a-difference-in-school-life

in Wales) is already threatening to marginalise other subjects including RE. With the revival of religion gathering pace it would be unwise for Christians to opt out of the state system at a time when there is more need than ever for Christian teachers, administrators and governors to defend the importance of religion in education.

While understanding the desire of some Christian parents to provide schooling for their children that is positively Christian this may not be the time for Christians to abandon the state system. There is growing pressure for a new settlement for religious education and the act of collective worship, especially from organisations such as the British Humanist Association and the National Secular Society. While Christians continue to have influence in education there is an opportunity to make the case for a religious education that teaches true tolerance - which means respect for those that have a different religion and their right to hold and express their faith freely. The state should not encourage the establishment of schools that do not uphold and teach these fundamental principles of a democratic state that respects the freedom of conscience. Insisting, with others, on such principles could be a valuable contribution by Christians to an education system that will build social cohesion and peace that is a crucial pre-requisite for evangelism.[26]

26 For a recent significant pamphlet on the future of RE and collective worship published in June 2015 by Westminster Faith Debates and available online see Charles Clarke and Linda Woodhead, *A New Settlement for RE in Schools.* See also Alan Dinham and Martha Shaw, *RE for Real*, Goldsmiths College London, 2015 - http://www.gold.ac.uk/media/goldsmiths/169-images/departments/research-units/faiths-unit/REforREal-web-b.pdf and also *Living with Difference: Community Diversity and the Common Good* a report of the Commission on Religion and Belief in British Public Life convened by the Woolf Institute, Cambridge and published Dec 2015 - http://corablivingwithdifference.com

To return to the 'Trojan Horse' letter - the problem in Birmingham lay with the failure of the local authority to uphold the values and principles of true tolerance that is fundamental in a democratic state. If the authority had carried out thorough inspections what was happening would have come to light. The fact that it was a group of Islamists that were trying to manipulate the governance system of some schools to propagate their particular brand of religion is irrelevant. If a group of fundamentalist Christians or Hindus tried to do the same it would have been just as contrary to the fundamental principles of education in a democratic state.

However, to conclude from this example of aberration that religion should be banished from state education would be as oppressive as allowing 'fundamentalists' to use the system for their own ends. With 59 per cent of the population of England and Wales saying that they were Christian in the 2011 Census to argue, as the British Humanist Association does, that it should be banished from school life except from an RE that simply provides information about what Christians believe seems undemocratic at best and oppressive at worst. Pupils in all schools should have an opportunity to learn about Christian beliefs and the implications of those beliefs for life. And in our multi-religious context this should be available in a context where pupils would have an opportunity to learn about the beliefs and lifestyle of other religions as well. As the dominant religious group, Trevor Cooling argues that Christians will need to exercise "courageous restraint" in order to do this:

*"The concept of 'courageous restraint' is one that invites particular attention as a replacement for the concept of dispassionate neutrality and its implied privatization of personal beliefs. Courageous restraint means that people are*

*willing to stand back from what is naturally their first priority in order to respect the integrity of other people. It means being willing to let fairness temper one's advocacy of truth as you understand it. It means holding to the golden rule that one should treat other people as you hope they would treat you in similar circumstances. It means being willing to accept that the truth you personally hold dear is contestable in wider society. For the teacher in the classroom it means welcoming the expression of points of view by pupils and in the syllabus that you personally think are flawed, sometimes fundamentally so. For curriculum developers it will mean not looking simply to champion your own particular view, but being willing to introduce diversity of views into a syllabus. For policy makers it will mean allowing developments that may personally be seen as retrograde. The adjective coura-geous to describe this restraint is appropriate because the investment of personal identity that people make in their beliefs is such that it does take courage to restrain oneself from seeking their advantage. The difference between cou-rageous restraint and neutrality is that the former does not treat personal beliefs as private and irrelevant. Rather it rec-ognizes their significant place in being human."[27]*

## Higher education

My teaching of undergraduates is now almost 30 years in the past. At that time the modularisation of higher education was just beginning. The process is well nigh complete by now. What this means is that 'subjects' are studied as a series of discrete modules. Added to this a package of modules from one subject can be supplemented with some modules from other subjects.

27   Trevor Cooling, *Doing God in Education*, op. cit. p. 63.

To illustrate what is happening, here is a possible route to a degree in religious and theological studies at Cardiff University. Each year a student has to build up a total of 180 credits and most courses are 20 credits:

**Year 1**
Two courses entitled 'An introduction to Religion' in which religion is studied through 'texts, poetry, film, biographies, fieldwork and drama.'

A course on 'The history of the Christian Church' and 'Introduction to the Bible'. This makes up 80 credits or two thirds of the first year's study.

The remaining 40 credits [two courses] can either be texts in their original languages – Sanskrit/Arabic/Hebrew/NT Greek or two modules from a wide range of other subjects such as philosophy, English, history, modern languages, politics, mathematics etc…

**Year 2**
In Year 2 the student will choose six out of more than 35 modules. Assuming that a student did not opt for texts in their original languages in the first year a second year diet could be the following:

Understanding Christian worship
Early Hinduism
Bodies, spirits and souls: the person, ethics and religion
Medieval church in the Latin west
Understanding Muslim scriptures
Christian Church today: its meaning, life and mission

**Year 3**

Since most modules are available in Years 2 and 3 the six chosen in Year 2 will reduce the choice at this stage. Here is a possible diet:

Beliefs in the crucible
Christian social ethics today
Buddhism, the first 1,000 years
Emotions, Symbols and rituals: studying societies through film
Ancient and medieval Judaism
Islam in the contemporary world

It is still possible in Cardiff and other universities to major on biblical studies by opting for the study of the biblical languages. However, it is only a small minority that opt for this route and most students opt for the sort of pick and mix route outlined above. This means that most students that leave university with a degree in religious and/or theological studies have only a very hazy conception of the structure of the theology of Christianity or any other religion.

Religious studies as a subject in universities was developed in the 1960s and 70s in the heyday of religious/theological pluralism and the legacy of that era persists although not as pervasive as it was. Having gone through a period of decline religious studies courses have grown in popularity in recent years. Probably because of the heavy influence of pluralism there have been very few evangelical scholars in religious studies departments. Those that are in the field come from the remnants of theology faculties that were populated by lecturers in theological colleges linked to universities. They may be able to make a contribution for some time yet but their presence is in decline and could disappear in the next 10 years.

What is needed is for evangelical scholars to seriously reconsider the contribution that universities ought to make in the field of RE. There can be no argument that universities have an obligation to teach about the religions that are practised by millions of British citizens. It is probably the case that the major world religions are fairly well-represented in university courses although it would be good to see more evangelical scholars in this area. Christianity is the one religion that is not that well-represented. With almost 60 per cent of the UK population choosing to call themselves Christian in the 2011 Census and so much of our history and culture having been shaped by Christianity the provision of the universities seems grossly inadequate.[28] What is needed is more scholars devoted to the study of Christianity as a religion rather than theological college lecturers linked to universities that can offer courses in some corner of the field of Christian studies that happens to be their research interest. Evangelical scholars would do well to equip themselves to be the interpreters of their religion and for their religion to be properly represented in university courses.

## Conclusion

The chapter began with a good example of how a religious group with strong convictions should not use the governance regime of state schools to push their agenda on a school. It would have been just as wrong for a group of fundamentalist evangelicals to do the same.

Meanwhile schools with a religious character have a legitimate and significant place in the UK education system. In the Church

---

28  The same can be said about RE in schools. From my experience pupils generally leave school with a very inadequate understanding of Christianity.

of England they are seen as an integral part of the mission of the Church but their responsibility to educate in a religiously plural context is also taken very seriously.

State-supported schools with a religious character should remain true to their religious roots that can be expressed in the teaching of the school but in such a way as not to undermine pupils from other religions.

While affirming a particular faith a school also has a responsibility to build peace – or social cohesion.

There are many evangelical Christians in the teaching profession. They should be valued and seen as 'missionaries' deserving encouragement and prayer support so that they can be good emissaries of Christ in what is often a very challenging situation.

Religious education remains as a compulsory subject in all UK schools. As evangelicals we agree that pupils should be introduced to the religions while at school.

The discussion is underway to develop a new settlement for RE and evangelicals need to be awake to this and make sure that their voice is heard. It is particularly important that the Christian tradition that has shaped the history and culture of the UK should be properly represented as the main component of any revised RE.

Historically RE teachers have been trained as theological pluralists and teach in a general school context dominated by the belief that religion is irrational. Research has now proved that pupils with strong religious convictions are intimidated and bullied by teachers and their peers.

**Church leaders and parents need to be conscious of the reality of religious bullying and draw this to the attention of schools. Christian governors can make sure that this type of bullying is included in school bullying policies.**

All schools are still required by law to hold an act of collective worship or religious observance (Scotland) for every pupil every day. The law is commonly ignored but while the law stands church leaders, youth workers and others are often welcome to help head teachers to keep the law.

Those involved in providing school assemblies should be sensitive to the religiously plural context of schools.

The existence of Christian schools is important as a reminder that ultimately the responsibility for a child's education lies with the parents. However, it would be a tragedy for Christians to withdraw from the state sector because the opportunity remains to influence the sector for good and to be a legitimate Christian voice in the public square – even if this means practising 'courageous restraint'.

Finally a case was made that the teaching of Christianity in higher education/universities is very deficient.

**There is a need for a deliberate attempt to foster evangelical scholars to teach in the religious studies sector and especially to teach Christianity as a religion.**

# CHAPTER 7

# Religions and politics[1]

*"Another issue that I think you need to be aware of is what I call the three great questions of the next twenty years. And I think these are questions that we're going to be facing — they're all religious issues — and here is what I think they are. Number one, will Islam modernize peacefully?"* Rick Warren[2]

Throughout history faith and religions have been intertwined with politics. Indeed, given the myth of secular neutrality, it could be argued that they are inseparable. Even so, historically they differ greatly in the way they relate to politics and government.

1  *Faith and Nation: Report of a Commission of Inquiry to the UK Evangelical Alliance*, 2006. This report deals with many of the issues raised in this chapter. It is available online at http://www.eauk.org/current-affairs/publications/upload/Faith-and-Nation.pdf

2  Rick Warren in an address to the US Ethics and Public Policy Center, May 2005 https://eppc.org/publications/rick-warren-at-the-may-2005-faith-angle-forum/

# Christianity

Christianity began as an alternative political reality to the Roman imperial rule that dominated the world in which Christianity emerged. 'Caesar is Lord' was the creed of Rome; 'Jesus is Lord' was the creed of the Christians. Christians were taught to deeply respect the state but they could never give it their absolute allegiance. Persecution was inevitable if sporadic for the first three centuries. Then the emperor Constantine became a Christian and from 313 AD the Church was shown favour by the state, eventually becoming the state religion of the Roman Empire during the reign of Theodosius (379-395). This led to the persecution of non-Christians and also of Christians that were considered heretical by the state. This close association between Christianity and the state became the prevailing model of both the Western and Eastern branches of the Roman Empire and was adopted by the states that were formed as the Roman Empire disintegrated.

As what became the European nations took shape Christianity became their official state-sponsored religion with the Western nations of the former Roman Empire looking to Catholic Rome and the Pope as the supreme Christian authority and the Eastern, mainly Slavic, nations looking to Orthodox Constantinople. Following the rapid spread of Islamic rule from the seventh century most Orthodox Christians were forced to live as disadvantaged minorities under Muslim rule. Despite this African and Middle Eastern Christianity flourished for centuries. Further east the non-Orthodox Nestorian and Jacobite churches also flourished establishing churches across Asia as far as China and living as minorities in non-Christian countries.[3]

---

3   For the story of the non-Western church see Philip Jenkins, *The Lost History of Christianity: The Thousand-Year Golden Age of the Church in the Middle East, Africa and Asia*, New York: Lion, 2008. This is an important book that has much to say to contemporary Muslims and Christians about a route to peaceful co-existence.

The creation of Christian states led to a long catalogue of terrible cruelty against Christians that deviated from the state orthodoxy and other religious minorities such as Jews and Muslims. It was not until the 17th century that some radical Puritans began to question the validity of using the power of the state to enforce a particular form of Christianity.

Roger Williams, the founder of Rhode Island in the US is probably the most famous. He argued that the state had no jurisdiction in matters of belief in God or gods. The state did not exist to force citizens into a particular form of religion but rather to keep the peace and restrain evildoers. People should be free to follow their conscience where belief in God was concerned. In Britain the idea of freedom of conscience became enshrined in English law in 1689 as a result of the Glorious Revolution that brought William of Orange to the English throne. In practice the Church of England remained in a privileged position after 1689 and other types of Protestant Christians had to contend with many disadvantages such as not being allowed to hold public office. It was not until well into the 19th century that all disadvantages were removed and that freedom of conscience was extended to include Roman Catholic Christians and adherents of other religions.

The Evangelical Alliance was formed in London in 1846 as the process of enshrining the idea of freedom of conscience in British law was nearing its completion. The primary motivation was to unite Christians from various denominations that were committed to spreading the gospel message of the Methodist revival. The other main object was "the defence and promotion of religious freedom". As Philip Schaff, who was a leading light in the Evangelical Alliance in the second half of the 19th century, states: "It is freedom as distinct from mere toleration, freedom of conscience as a fundamental and unalienable right of every man, and freedom of worship, which is the natural result of the former, and which the government is bound to protect."[4] This commitment to the religious freedom of Christians is even expressed in the second clause of the 1846 Alliance Doctrinal Basis: "The right and duty of private judgment in the interpretation of Holy Scriptures."

This commitment led to successful lobbying by the Alliance particularly on behalf of non-Roman Catholics in southern Europe. Another significant success was its contribution to the movement that induced the Sultan of Turkey to abolish the death penalty for apostasy from Islam in 1856.

It is right to weep because of the terrible atrocities that have been perpetrated by state-sponsored Christianity but also to rejoice that the evangelical movement that found expression in the formation of the Evangelical Alliance has consistently stood for religious freedom. The Evangelical Alliance in the UK still treasures this freedom that is still frequently violated and much of its public policy work is geared to protecting it. In February 2015 the Alliance together with Release International, Christian Solidarity Worldwide and Open Doors launched the UK Religious Liberty Commission.[5] The World Evangelical Alliance also has a Religious Liberty Commission and established an International Institute for Religious Freedom that publishes well-researched material on breaches of religious freedom in different countries. A case has been made that 76 per cent of

---

4   *A Religious Encyclopaedia*, ed. Philip Schaff, 3rd ed., London: Funk and Wagnalls, 1894, vol. 1, p. 60

5   The commission's web presence is hosted by the Evangelical Alliance website at www.eauk.org/rlc

states now impose some restrictions on religious freedom so the need for such bodies is greater than ever.

This legacy should give the Alliance significant credibility as the UK seeks to understand afresh religious freedom in light of the influx of adherents of religions that do not share our history.

# Hinduism

Hinduism emerged among the peoples of India. It contains many strands, developed over long periods and in different regions. The word 'Hindu' was originally a geographical term used by the Persians to describe the people of the Indus river region. Later Muslim invaders called the region Hindustan, the country of the people of Hind/Sind. In the 18th and 19th centuries the term 'Hinduism' was coined to describe the religions, customs, culture and way of life of the peoples of India. In this sense Hinduism could be described as a 'national' religion. It certainly belongs to the land of India with its devotion strongly linked to topography with its rivers, especially the Ganges, being especially sacred.

Where beliefs are concerned Hinduism is more like a network of religions than a single unified set of beliefs. It is bewilderingly variegated with many gods worshipped and rituals observed under the umbrella of a belief in a cosmic, moral and social order [*dharma*].

The diversity of belief and practice that developed in India predisposes the Hindu tradition to tolerance. Traditionally the Hindu system is able to absorb new beliefs and practices. Its real strength lies in its social system of family and community. This is probably one of the many reasons for its survival despite the fact that much of India was dominated by other religious traditions such as Buddhism and Islam for much of its history. Even though Buddhism and especially Islam came with strong state support, and vicious persecution at times in the case of the latter, Hinduism was not rooted out. When these religions lost their grip on power the more ancient Hindu tradition re-asserted itself again.

British rule posed a different threat. Though by the beginning of the 19th century British rule was officially supporting the establishing of Christianity in India it did so within a legal framework that endorsed the freedom of religion. The arrangement that was in place in the UK by 1850 was replicated in India. The Church of England was the state church but there was freedom for adherents of non-Anglican Christian groups and of the Hindu and other religions to practice and propagate their faith.

At independence in 1947 the principle of religious freedom was enshrined in law in the Indian Constitution. India was defined as a 'secular' state, not in the common sense of the absence of religion but of the equality of all religions without privileging any one of them. However, in the two decades before independence a Hindu nationalist movement was formed that advocated the privileging of Hinduism in India. This movement has grown since independence and the current prime minister of India heads the Bharatiya Janata Party (BJP) that is a strongly nationalist party renowned for advocating opposition to minority religions in India – especially Islam and Christianity. The BJP has supported the passing of anti-conversion laws in a number of Indian states and radical Hindu groups such as the Rashtriya Swayamsevak Sangh (RSS) use these laws to foment attacks against Christians. The worse attack so far was in Orissa in 2008 when 100 Christians were killed and around 50,000 people were displaced. While there has been no attack on that scale since, the Evangelical Fellowship of India are, sadly, reporting cases of harassment of Christians such as beatings, destruction of church property and violent accusations of unlawful conversion on a regular basis. Some Christians are also killed in these attacks.

The Hinduism that has led to persecution of other religions – especially Christianity and Islam - was born out of a nationalist reaction to foreign rule in India. It asserts that to be Indian is to belong to the religious traditions that have developed in India, which includes the Sikh and Buddhist traditions. Therefore, other religious traditions have no place in India.

Because this persecuting Hindu movement is very much focused on India it is not likely to have a great impact on the lives of Hindus in the UK. Hindus here are more likely to emphasise the tolerant and accommodating nature of their faith. However, the impact of the Hindu nationalist movement may strengthen reaction against the perceived imposition of Western values on the Hindu tradition – as perceived by some. This was exemplified in recent responses to what was said about the caste system in the House of Lords.

In March 2013 Lord Harries of Prendergast, the former Bishop of Oxford, introduced an amendment to the Enterprise and Regulatory Reform Bill to include caste discrimination as an offence alongside race discrimination. The Lords passed the amendment but the debate caused uproar among some Hindus and Sikhs. The Lords were attacked for their lack of understanding and for their colonial approach. Because an Anglican bishop moved the amendment, Hindus and Sikhs were also able to speak of an attack on them from the Church of England establishment.[6]

---

6    See www.nchtuk.org for a taste of the Hindu reaction, in particular this response video featuring on their home page: https://www.youtube.com/watch?v=z5-XQdinqHo (sites accessed 08 November 2016)

It is very unlikely that Hindus will want to restrict the freedom of other religions in the UK. Their concern is to be treated as full members of British society so that their voice will be heard by government as much as the voice of other religions.

# Sikhism

The Sikh religion is the youngest of the religions under consideration in this resource. Its source is the life and teaching of Guru Nanak (1469-1539). Nanak was in many ways a typical Indian/Hindu holy man who discovered a way to the divine and having gained a reputation as a holy man attracted followers that he was able to initiate into his way. What he did was to fuse aspects of the devotion to a deity [*bhakti*] tradition in India and the Sufi tradition of Islam. From Hinduism he took the belief in reincarnation and some *bhakti* devotional practices such as repetition of the divine name and from Sufi Islam he took monotheism and a rejection of caste. Nanak was succeeded by nine gurus whose work was gathered together into the holy book of Sikhism – the Guru Granth Sahib.

Nanak was a pacifist but historical circumstances eventually turned his followers from pacifists to being renowned for their military prowess. The change came with the 10th guru Gobind Singh who taught that Sikhs could take up the sword to defend themselves against Muslim aggression. Gobind Singh was responsible for establishing the Khalsa – the Sikh order that take the five symbols as their marks of Sikh identity. One of the symbols was a sword.

Under the leadership of the Maharaja Ranjit Singh, who died in 1839, many Sikhs were united into one kingdom centred in Lahore. By this time to be a Sikh meant belonging to the Punjabi Sikh nation as much as following a particular religious path. That

Sikhs see themselves as an ethnic as well as a religious group is illustrated by the controversy caused by the 2011 Census form. The Office of National Statistics (ONS) decided to include 'Sikh' in the list of religion options that could be voluntarily ticked. The UK Sikh Foundation strongly objected to this arguing that 'Sikh' should be an option in the ethnicity part of the form. They also argued that not to include Sikh as an ethnic identity would lead to the Sikh community in the UK being considered a lot smaller than it actually is. Since the ONS refused to change the form Sikhs now maintain with some justification that they are a much larger community than the 2011 Census says they are.

As a nation the Sikhs have suffered much. They were oppressed by the Mughal emperors, divided by the British, torn apart by the partition of India at independence in 1947 and divided again by the government of independent India. When they fought for their independence from India they were brutally suppressed by Indira Gandhi's forces. It is not surprising that they are keen to preserve their identity and that they have succeeded in getting the UK government to recognise that they are different. For example, a turbaned Sikh does not have to wear a helmet to ride a motorbike like everyone else.

Sikhs have benefited from the policy of multiculturalism that has dominated government policy towards ethnic minorities since the 1960s. Many have kept their identity. Like the Hindus they desire to be treated equally as a religious and ethnic community but are unlikely to want to see British society as a whole re-created in their image.

## Buddhism

The founder of Buddhism, Siddhartha Gautama, who lived on the border of India and Nepal in the fifth century BC, was reputedly a prince who aged 29 forsook his position and family to seek enlightenment. Having become the Buddha, which means 'the enlightened one', he spent the rest of his life teaching his disciples, many of whom chose to follow him in his path of mendicant monasticism. Buddhism, therefore, was founded and developed without the support of state power.

Buddhism was a missionary religion from the beginning and it spread through much of south-east Asia without the aid of state patronage. This is not surprising since non-violence is a fundamental Buddhist doctrine. Over time Buddhism did gain state patronage such as by Ashoka, the third century BC. Mauryan emperor who ruled over most of India. He promoted the teaching of the Buddha but did not force people to adopt Buddhism or persecute those that chose other religious paths. In other countries such as Sri Lanka and Myanmar where Buddhism came to be tightly woven into the social fabric, a persecuting Buddhism has been born – especially when the traditional Buddhist way has been threatened by missionary religions such as Christianity and Islam.

There are no great concentrations of immigrants from traditionally Buddhist countries in the UK. There are enough here and there to sustain temples or centres that represent national Buddhism such as that of Sri Lanka or Tibet. But because of its history the Buddhist community is not going to demand attention from the state like other religious communities. The danger for evangelical Christians is that we will ignore the Buddhist presence in our midst. Buddhism has not lost its missionary edge and a significant number are attracted to its offer of a religious reality that does not demand belief in god.

# Judaism

In the Old Testament the religion of Israel was a national religion but from New Testament times until 1948 the descendants of Judah/Benjamin – who became known as the Jews – existed without the protection of a state they could call their own. Despite this they survived and spread out into many parts of the world. They had spread to many parts of the Roman Empire even before the time of Christ. Wherever they went they were eventually persecuted, although they did eventually find a safe haven in the Americas, especially the US. Since their terrible treatment at the hands of the Nazis they also have a safe haven in Europe – although anti-Semitism still rears its ugly head at times.

Amid great controversy the state of Israel was founded in 1948 in order to give Jews protection from persecution. Founded as a secular state with religious freedom, it has been a militarised society from the outset due to security threats. The Palestinian community that was displaced by it, who refuse to accept the Jewish state or their displacement, oppose its existence, as do a range of Islamist groups. The foundation of the state of Israel and the displacement of the mainly Muslim Palestinians has political ramifications way beyond the Middle East as we shall see in the section on Islam in this chapter.

In the UK they embrace the principle of religious freedom and the policy of multiculturalism that grants them considerable freedom to be what they want to be. Hasidic Jews sometimes fall foul of liberal Western values, such as when Hasidic mothers were forbidden from driving their children to school, but on the whole they are allowed to order their lives as they choose.

As a national religion, to be ethnically Jewish is to be religiously Jewish. Although secular or atheistic Jews don't believe in the

God of the Old Testament they often observe Jewish religious customs. This means that Jews by definition cannot be Christians or adherents of any other religion. Strictly speaking even Messianic Jews are a contradiction in terms. Not surprisingly Jews object strongly to any attempt to convert them to Christ and often equate any such attempt with the persecution that they have suffered in the past.

## Islam

Islam has been intertwined with political power from the beginning. Muslims claim that Muhammad started receiving messages from God about 610 AD when he was around 40 and continued to receive messages until his death in 632 AD. In 622 AD, having failed to persuade the people of Mecca that he was a prophet, he migrated with his followers to Medina where he had been invited to become their ruler. Muslims date the beginning of their religion from this move to take the reins of government of the town of Medina. Muhammad continued to persuade fellow Arabs as well as Jews and Christians that he was a prophet of God but the hostility of the Meccans meant that, from the time of the move to Medina/Yathrib, Islam spread by force of arms as well as verbal persuasion.

Islam means 'submission' and historically the submission expected was not only to God but also to Islamic rule that became embodied in the Islamic legal system of *shari'a*. Historically living under a Muslim government is the default position of Islam on the relationship between the religion and the state. Most Muslims have historically lived in states in which Muslim law prevailed. This has meant that:

1  The religion of polytheists in particular has been proscribed and adherents persecuted.

2 Christians and Jews, because they were regarded as having received a genuine revelation - embodied in a book – were allowed to practise their religion. However, they were given a second-class status by being subjected to special taxes and having their freedom limited in various ways. They were strictly forbidden from making converts of Muslims. These disadvantages did not stop the Church and Jewish communities from surviving for many centuries under Muslim rule and in the case of the Church establishing mission churches deep into Asia and Africa.[7]

3 For much of Muslim history apostasy from Islam was considered a crime punishable by death. Such a law is not found in the Qur'an but in one strand of the traditions of the first four generations (Hadith). Some Muslim dominated states, such as Turkey, have turned their back on this practice in favour of more freedom of religion. In some states the law is seldom applied even if still theoretically binding. Many contemporary Islamists believe that the death penalty for apostasy should be applied in an ideal Muslim state. In some countries where this law is not applied the families of converts sometimes take the law into their own hands and kill their apostate relative.

The expansion of the great European colonial empires – especially the British Empire – had a profound impact on Islam. In India millions of Muslims found themselves ruled by administrations that advocated religious freedom, which meant a substantial loss of status and privilege. British influence also extended to Afghanistan and Iran and after the First World

---

7  Philip Jenkins op. cit. tells the amazing story of Christian missionary expansion from Muslim dominated lands.

War, with France and the US, into much of the Middle East and Egypt. Ironically in the Middle East imperial power bolstered traditional repressive regimes in countries such as Iran, Iraq and Syria that were opposed by indigenous Westernised socialist movements in the name of democracy.

While much of the Middle East was in turmoil Arabia had become a paradigm of Muslim stability under the royal house of Saud. In the 18th century the house of Saud adopted the views of Muhammad ibn Abd al-Wahhab (1703–1792). He was a purist that advocated going back to original Islam. His severe monotheism rejected the veneration of Muslim saints – including Muhammad himself. A traditional Muslim penal code was adhered to. Since the 19th century Wahhabism has been the official religion of Saudi Arabia. In the 1970s Saudi Arabia became fabulously wealthy as a result of the oil crisis and since then it has invested billions of dollars annually in exporting its Wahhabi – or Salafi – brand of Islam all over the world.

Turning to the colonial empires, as the movement for independence from colonial rule gathered momentum Muslims grasped at the opportunity to return to their privileged position as dominating majorities. The best example of this is the division of the Indian Empire into India and Pakistan. Though East Pakistan broke away to become Bangladesh in 1971 both Pakistan and Bangladesh are states in which Muslims are a dominant majority. Both Pakistan and Bangladesh have a democratic constitution with religious freedom guaranteed in law but the Islamic renewal of the last quarter of the 20th century is pushing the countries towards the adoption of *shari'a*.

The mass immigration of Muslims to the UK also happened after independence and is largely the result of conflict. The chaos caused by the partition of the Indian Empire led many to migrate from the divided Punjab region. Many Bangladeshis from the Sylhet district migrated to the UK in the 1970s after the civil war in 1971. A significant proportion also came from East Africa having been driven out by Jomo Kenyatta and Idi Amin. The chaos in Somalia led to the dramatic growth of the Somali community in the UK and currently the civil war is causing many Syrians to knock at the UK's door.

A significant proportion also came to take advantage of the economic opportunities being offered by the British government in the 1950s and 60s. A large proportion of those that took advantage of this opportunity came from Mirpur in Kashmir.

The overwhelming majority of Muslims that have come to the UK in the last 60 years came with no thought of making the UK a Muslim country. They came because having experienced British rule in the colonial era they believed that they could have a better life in the UK. When they arrived many suffered discrimination and rejection but from the 1960s successive governments have affirmed their right to retain and foster their cultural identity so that as the number of immigrants grew, with large concentrations in the cities, they were able to enjoy the economic advantages of being in the UK while remaining culturally Pakistani or Bangladeshi. Since being Muslim was a central aspect of their cultural identity the places they live have become very obviously Islamic as we saw in the introduction.

The growth of the Muslim presence in the cities has happened at the same time as the re-awakening of Islam, especially in its heartland in the Middle East, and south and south-east Asia. Muslim communities in the UK have retained strong links with their countries of origins. Most of their religious teachers have been born and trained in Pakistan. It is inevitable that this Muslim revival has come to the UK. The increasing number of women in hijab and niqab on our city streets is the most obvious evidence that this is the case.

A significant proportion of UK Muslims are now Islamists.[8] Islamists work towards Muslim domination of states and the imposition of Muslim law [*shari'a*] on all. In countries like the UK it means working towards giving Muslims a privileged status beyond criticism. This is why some Muslims in the UK respond with such vehemence to any perceived insult or criticism. Conditioning the general population never to question the rightness of anything Muslim is a first step in the direction of Muslim domination.

The most extreme manifestation of this re-awakening is the radical arm of the Islamist movement. The focus of radical Islamists is on the worldwide Muslim community (the *ummah*). Central to their ideology is the perceived injustice done to their Palestinian brothers as a result of founding the state of Israel. Since Israel was established and survives because of Western military backing – particularly from the US – their hatred of the West is almost as profound as their hatred of Israel. The failure of the West to protect their Muslim brothers in Bosnia-Herzegovina and Kosovo confirmed their prejudices and their belief that Muslims need to take up arms to defend themselves – that violent *jihad* is the only option.

The chaos created by the invasion of Iraq and the civil war in Syria created the perfect context to bring together the ideal of

---

8   Some, such as Ed Hussain, say that the majority of Muslims are Islamists, Ed Husain, *The Islamist*, London, Penguin Books, 2007, pp. 165-167

violent jihad and the eschatological belief that in the end times a perfect Muslim state (caliphate) would emerge led by the ideal Muslim ruler (caliph). This is what IS (Islamic State) claims to be and hundreds of mainly young men and women from the UK have welcomed this development and gone to Syria or Iraq so that they can be a part of what they perceive as the ideal Muslim society. But most radical Islamists in the UK have not accepted IS's claims. Hizb ut Tahrir shares IS's conviction that re-establishing the Caliphate is vital for the future of Islam but rejects IS's sectarianism. They believe that Islam needs a model Islamic society in which a caliph would uphold *sharia'h* and in which all types of Muslims as well as Christians and Jews would live. Their recent series of conferences on the caliphate in the UK attracted thousands of participants.

There is also evidence that the Islamist movement is having a significant impact among young Muslims in the UK. A recent survey by Policy Exchange found that 36 per cent of Muslims in the 16 to 24 age bracket approved of the death penalty for apostasy.[9]

Since the radical Islamists are very anti-Western and execrate the Western form of democratic government they are a threat to religious freedom. However, their focus is not usually on the UK but on establishing an ideal Muslim government in a country where Muslims are already in the majority. In the UK the challenge is more visible through other Islamist groups which are specifically focused on seeing the UK become more and more Islamic.

---

9  "Policy Exchange, 'Living apart together: British Muslims and the paradox of multiculturalism' available at: https://www.policyexchange.org.uk/wp-content/uploads/2016/09/living-apart-together-jan-07.pdf"

# Evangelicals, the religions and politics

## Immigrants in the Old Testament

The Old Testament talks of two types of immigrants – the *gēr* and the *nokrī*.

*Gērîm* [pl.of *gēr*] were people who came to live among the Israelites because they became convinced that the Israelite way of life was superior. This motivation continues to apply to most immigrants to the United Kingdom today. The two main reasons for immigration are seeking refuge from persecution and the hope of a better economic opportunity. Most immigrants would not have moved without coming to the conclusion that life would be better for them in a place where the culture differed from their own. So, for many, immigration involves at least a presumption of a measure of assimilation into another culture.

In the Greek Septuagint translation of the Old Testament *gēr* is always translated *proselytos* [proselyte, convert]. This confirms the presumption of assimilation or integration and explains the very inclusive legislation concerning the *gērîm*.

They were not to be ill-treated (Exodus 22:21-22; Leviticus 19:33; Psalm 146:9; Zechariah 7:10).

They were to be loved (Leviticus 19:34).

They were to be included (Leviticus 19:10; 23:22; Deuteronomy 16:11,14; 24:19-21).

The *nokrî* were immigrants who considered their former way of life as superior and, therefore, insisted on retaining their national culture and did everything in their power to persuade others in their adopted country to assimilate to their way of life. They saw immigration as an opportunity to subvert their host culture.

Typical examples of this type of immigrant in the Old Testament were some of the foreign wives that Solomon married and Ahab's Sidonian wife Jezebel. In the case of Naboth's vineyard Jezebel was able to insinuate into Israel a way of exercising power that was totally opposed to what God had revealed to the Israelites.[10]

It is almost certain that the Hindu, Sikh, Buddhist and Muslim immigrants that came to the UK in the 50s and 60s of the last century came as *gerim*. Why then are many of their children and grandchildren, especially among Muslims, becoming *nokri*? One possible answer is that there has been a failure of love, kindness and inclusion on the part of citizens of the UK. Much damage has already been done but it is never too late for Christians – and evangelical Christians in particular – to be loving, kind and inclusive.

Fear must be cast aside and contact made with the leaders of the religious communities in our area. Evangelical churches are already doing much to reach out but engaging with leaders is vital. By doing this it may be possible for people from various religions to work together for the benefit of their community as a whole. It is only through respectful contact that issues such as the freedom of religion can be discussed.

## *Freedom to convert*

The freedom to convert is fundamental to religious freedom.

Jim Stewart is the National Assembly liaison officer for the Evangelical Alliance in Wales. His engagement with the Faith Communities Forum that meets with the first minister on a

10 See Dewi Hughes, *Power and Poverty: Divine and Human Rule in a World of Need*, (Nottingham: IVP, 2008), pp. 72-73.

regular basis has led to serious inter-religious discussion about conversion:

Jim's story:

"My first exposure to interfaith meetings came when I joined the Faith Communities Forum of the Welsh Assembly after starting work for the Evangelical Alliance in Wales in 2005. Forum meetings were interesting and clearly served a purpose, leading for example to respectful relationships at a national level between leaders of different faiths in Wales. However, I soon realised that such forums were not the best place to discuss sensitive issues. For example, the issue of religious conversion never came up on the agenda.

This particular issue was of interest to me and, curious to know what the experiences were of Christians in Wales who had converted from a Muslim background, I accessed some funding in 2012 to have a report written. Katie, who had written a dissertation on apostasy in Muslim-majority countries for her international relations Masters, interviewed 15 Muslim-background believers (MBBs) in south Wales from various ethnic backgrounds and wrote a report on her findings.

From the report, which confirmed our hunch that the religious freedom of some MBBs had not been respected, I gave presentations to Welsh government, South Wales Police, the Welsh Refugee Council and others.

Although these presentations were helpful in raising awareness, I felt that there were other aspects to this issue that I hadn't yet grasped. Upon reflection, I realised that Muslims themselves were not really engaged in the issue, and began to think of ways of getting them engaged. If some Muslims were part of the problem, then they also had to be part of the solution.

As a result I organised an event for interfaith week in November 2013 entitled 'Welcoming the convert'. I tried to develop a neutral language for talking about this issue that didn't alienate people. For example, I said in the poster that converts were vulnerable because they might not be fully accepted by their new faith community and were distanced from the one they had left behind. If this was the case we needed to understand their experiences and ensure that they were supported. The event had the support of six Muslim organisations and provided two perspectives - one a Welsh Muslim from a Christian background and the other a Welsh-Iranian Christian from a Muslim background. There were 20 people present and the discussions were respectful and enlightening, with no one trying to score points for their faith.

Currently I'm working on the next phase of this journey, which is a joint-statement for Christian and Muslim leaders to sign, supporting the right of the individual to choose their faith. This has the support of some imams in Cardiff who have welcomed it.

Some of the salient points for me in this journey have been:
- The advantage of having the Welsh Assembly and Welsh government hosting the Faith Communities Forum. This provides an incentive for people to engage in such issues as to not do so could result in a loss of face.

- There are a number of different lenses through which this issue can be seen. I choose to approach it through a commitment to religious freedom for all, working as a peacemaker towards a future of peaceful co-existence between people of different faiths and none. I want to see Christianity flourishing in Wales but I can still be an authentic Christian while working for religious freedom for all.

- I try to be wise in my use of social media. Sometimes we can post articles that really only speak to people who think like us, and don't accomplish much in the way of bridge building.

I have been pleased with the way that our work on religious conversion has developed, not least in managing to elicit the support of Muslims and engage Welsh government. Praise must be given to God at the outset, however, as I have always felt that this initiative could only be done in and through Him.

Having devolved government in Wales, and thus decision-making closer to the people, has been helpful. It has meant that I have been able to raise religious conversion as an agenda item through the Faith Communities Forum, a body that meets twice a year with Wales' first minister. Recently I received positive feedback that the Welsh government sees this initiative as something that promotes diversity and inclusiveness. That in itself is insightful and has given me an idea of how to promote the project if I want to see further engagement from public sector bodies.

The involvement of some Muslim groups has developed over time. First, at a national level in Wales, an almost symbiotic relationship has developed among the different faith leaders via engagement through bodies such as the Faith Communities Forum, mentioned above. This has been shaped in part by government and other public bodies relating to us primarily as faith groups rather than seeing us first and foremost as individual faiths. Also many of the issues in public life that have been of concern to Christians in recent years (e.g. same-sex marriage, proposed changes to religious education) have also been shared by most if not all of the other faiths. As a result, we have often seen each other as allies on issues and shared information. Moreover we have tended to support each other in times of difficulty, as was the case in 2010 when faith leaders led peace vigils in response to anti-Muslim marches organised by the English Defence League. These gestures were very much appreciated by Muslim leaders at the time.

As a result, Muslim willingness to engage on the issue of religious conversion has probably stemmed in part from a combination of these factors above.

However, I also feel that there is a genuine desire among some Muslims to lend their support to causes such as freedom to convert because they believe that there should be no compulsion in religion and also to show that Islam and western democracy are not mutually incompatible.

Finally, the involvement of Welsh government acts as an incentive for Muslims and other groups to get involved because of the associated prestige[11] - and possible loss of face for not doing so.[12]

## Multiculturalism

As stated in the introduction multiculturalism was established as government policy in 1966 when Roy Jenkins was the Labour

---

11  Support from a local MP would have a similar effect.

12  For more details of this journey and lessons learned, please see the following article that appeared in a recent edition of the Evangelical Alliance's *idea* magazine - http://www.eauk.org/idea/welcoming-the-convert.cfm

home secretary. He described what was then a new approach as 'integration'. This meant rejecting "a flattening process of assimilation' in favour of 'equal opportunity, coupled with cultural diversity, in an atmosphere of mutual tolerance".[13] In the context of the racism suffered by so many immigrants that arrived in the 1950s and 60s this policy was a breath of fresh air. It affirmed the need to make sure that immigrants were given as good an opportunity as anyone to prosper, that they had freedom to be culturally different so that communities of immigrant origin would be able to live in good relations with their host society/country and vice versa. The aim was 'integration' (unity in diversity) rather than 'assimilation' (uniformity).

Since the Bradford riots of 2001, 9/11 and 7/7 the policy of multiculturalism has come under intense scrutiny. Not surprisingly the Muslim community, because of its size and concentration in many inner city, has come under the most intense spotlight. As a result government policy has switched focus from racism and equal opportunities to social cohesion, which is understood in terms of assimilation to 'British' cultural values. Some like Jenny Bourne in her paper 'In Defence of Multiculturalism' for the Institute of Race Relations wants to return to the focus on justice, racism and civil rights as a champion of the Muslim community. Her only reference to religion is to attack the Christian supporters of social cohesion: "They essentially want British culture to be more traditional and/or Christianity to prevail over other faiths."[14]

Every Christian should support any struggle against racism and should be in the vanguard of most struggles for justice and civil

13  Jenkins quoted in S. Poulter, *Ethnicity, Law and Human Rights*, Oxford Univ. Press, 1998, p.15-18.

14  Jenny Bourne, *In Defence of Multiculturalism*, Institute of Race Relations Briefing Paper, No. 2, p. 2

rights so we have no problem with Bourne's viewpoint on this front. What is surprising is that she does not seem to grasp that Muslims have a religion and that their religion is very central to the life of many of them. If those Christians that want Christianity to prevail in the UK are criticised for their religious beliefs in the debate about racism etc then surely questions need to be asked about the Muslim's religious vision of the future/futures of the UK. Since the populations of immigrant origin are the most religious communities in the UK, if multiculturalism is to have a future at all, then the religious dimension must be central to any progress towards integration.[15]

What was reported at the death of Hafiz Mohammad Patel, the leader of the Tablighi Jamaat in Britain in February 2016 amply testifies to the need for religious discussion to be at the heart of any attempt to foster a peaceful multicultural society. The report in the Lapido Media e-newsletter says that: "Tablighi Jamaat has attempted to create segregated societies in which Tablighi Muslims can live separate from the mainstream of British society. [As Sikand notes]: 'The Tablighi ethos works to minimize contact with people of other faiths, withdrawing from the wider society to protect Islam from the threat of secularism and materialism'".[16]

Tablighi Jamaat has many thousands of followers and worked hard for years to get planning permission to build the biggest mosque and Muslim centre in Europe in Newham in London. It was probably a good understanding of their separatist religious

---

15 Jenny Taylor's research proved that government began to recognize this in the 1990s. See *After Secularism: Inner-City Governance and the New religious Discourse,* London, SOAS, 2002

16 Zacharias Pieri, 'What now for Tablighi Jamaat after death of leader?', Lapido Media e-newsletter, February 21, 2016. Available at http://www.lapidomedia.com/node/6583

stance that led the council to succeed in turning them down on the grounds that their plan would not benefit the whole community of Newham.

The positivist belief that all religion was destined to dwindle and die before the inexorable progress of materialist science's ability to solve all human problems became ascendant in British intellectual circles by the middle of the 20th century. Religion could still be allowed as a private affair but it was banished from the public square. Politics and social planning – even foreign policy – could do without any understanding of religion. It was assumed that the primitive irrational thinking represented by religion couldn't possibly contribute to progress in society so it was safe to ignore it.[17] Any rational assessment of what has happened in Britain and the Middle East in the last 10 years testifies that the opposite is the case. It is becoming more and more obvious that religion cannot be confined to the private realm and that religious understanding is vital for all who work for the good of society.

Lapido Media, referred to above, was set up to make up the deficit of religious knowledge and understanding in the media. It's an organisation "founded by journalists to advocate for greater awareness of the faith dimension in policy, governance, and conflict in the UK and abroad". Its founder is Jenny Taylor, an evangelical Christian.

## Conclusion

Religion and politics are always intertwined. In the UK, while playing their part in our party political life, Sikhs and Jews are

---

17  Alistair Campbell's famous response to a question about Tony Blair's faith, 'We don't do God!' encapsulates the positivist approach.

particularly concerned that government provides the legal framework for preserving their religio-ethnic identity. Hindus likewise are happy to play their part in public life but are very concerned to preserve their communitarian heritage. Muslims are more ambivalent. There are many that are fully integrated into the UK political heritage of democracy and religious freedom. There are others that are happy to work within the system in order to subvert it in favour of the ultimate domination of Islam over the whole of UK politics. There are others that stand aloof in pursuit of a purist Islam and a few that have come to hate the system so much that they are prepared to become suicide bombers or leave to join jihadist groups.

Christians in the UK are inheritors of the vestiges of Christianity as the official religion of the state and of the institutionalisation of religious freedom. From its foundation in 1846 religious freedom has been a cherished principle and central preoccupation of the Evangelical Alliance. In the context of the religions there is increasing need to defend and propagate the principle of religious freedom.

The right to convert is fundamental to religious freedom. Hinduism is the religion most opposed to conversion although they have not as yet sought to campaign for anti-conversion laws in the UK as have been legislated in a number of Indian states. Muslims work hard to see people converted to Islam and many strongly oppose those that convert out of Islam.

The Old Testament speaks of immigrants as either *gerim* or *nokri* – those who want to integrate into or subvert their host culture. If adherents of the religions are not to become *nokri* then it is vital to engage with them on the issue of religious freedom. In the political context one obvious way to do this is to engage with the Inter-faith Forums that are being formed at local and national levels. The Evangelical Alliance Wales involvement with the Welsh Assembly Inter-faith Forum has opened the way to serious Muslim-Christian discussion about the right to convert.

As evangelicals committed to religious freedom it is vital that we seek opportunities to talk directly to representatives of the religions. Inter-faith Forums is an obvious place to begin.

The most serious hindrance to community peace-building in the UK has been the banishment of religion from the public square. We should rejoice that the presence of the religions among the immigrant populations[18] is forcing government to abandon this untenable position.

We must make sure that the Christian voice is heard as the voice of the religions becomes more significant in discussions about integration.

The banishment of religion from the public square for more than a generation means that those who guide the public dialogue such as journalists and public servants at all levels are often woefully ignorant of the religions.

**As evangelicals we have a duty to make sure that opinion formers and public servants have a better understanding of Christianity and the religions.**

---

18 Including the strong presence of Christianity among the black immigrant population.

# Afterword

## Dr David Landrum, director of advocacy, Evangelical Alliance

Religion is problematic. There are few biblical references to it, and most are negative. For those who have a personal relationship with the living God, the cross exposes the human limitations of religion in the light of God's grace. In Christ, the law is fulfilled. God has done it all. Our response is to believe and receive. As such, Christianity is not simply one among many other religions, but differs from all others in that its content is divinely revealed and its outward expression by believers is not an attempt to secure salvation but a thank-offering.[1]

Even so, despite the incompatibilities of religion and Christianity, we need a word to describe mankind's expression of an acknowledgement of the divine – and the practices and paraphernalia that go with it. With this qualification, the 'religions' represent important spheres for Christian mission and church engagement globally.

Religion and Christianity are resurgent. So much so that Peter Berger's famous secularisation thesis has now become the de-secularisation thesis. In the UK, notwithstanding the

---

1   See: *New Bible Dictionary – Second Edition* (1994), IVP, Leicester, p1017

paradox of secularism being both ascendant and collapsing, the landscape of religion and belief is also changing dramatically.

Whereas once we could rest on the cultural assumptions of Christendom, as with the early Church, we are now confronted by the challenges of a society characterised by religious plurality. Whereas once, we strove to assimilate newcomers to a generic Christian milieu, now, Christians are now faced with pressures to acquiesce to a prevailing liberal imperialism. In this context, to self-identify as a Bible-believing follower of Jesus comes with a cost. Maybe, as it should?

Much has been written in recent years about the decline of Christian Britain, and although 'cultural Christianity' may be fading fast, more authentic forms of faith are going from strength to strength. Evangelicals, whether described as charismatic, conservative, reformed or Pentecostal, are prominent in this displacement of nominal, lukewarm Christianity. For some, this stripping away of the veneer of indigenous religious homogeneity is disconcerting, particularly when accompanied by the increasing public visibility of religions other than Christianity. For others, the situation provides new and exciting evangelistic opportunities. Today, as Christians rub shoulders with many other religious identities in the UK, two key challenges face evangelicals. The first relates to mission – how we reach adherents of other religions with the life-bringing message of salvation in the Lord Jesus Christ. The second relates to society – how we can live together with our deepest differences.

In this context, it's important for the mission of God, that evangelicals are better equipped and more confident to engage with those of other religions. The careful theological reflections and practical suggestions in this resource help with this task.

From a solid biblical basis it provides for a clearer understanding of the nature of the religions and also the dynamics of the project of multiculturalism that has fostered cultural pluralism.

Crucially, the book shows how, when engaging with adherents of other religions, the gospel imperative needs to be the central driver for evangelicals. Without this we lack distinctiveness, authenticity and purpose. It's our USP – what makes us evangelicals. As Tim Keller notes:

> "If we confuse evangelism and social justice we lose what is the single most unique service that Christians can offer the world. Others, alongside believers, can feed the hungry. But Christians have the gospel of Jesus by which men and women can be born into a certain hope of eternal life. No one else can make such an invitation."[2]

In order to be faithful to God's mission, and also to play our part in an authentically plural public square, our engagement with people of other religions should be distinctive. It should be notably, visibly, confidently Christian. Innovation and creativity will always be important for cross-cultural mission, but in the long-run, in a society marked more by novelty than sincerity, it will be the strength of our convictions that will secure the enduring respect of the other. Needless to say, as the resource confirms, such a transparent mode of engagement must be framed by grace, especially when dealing with core doctrines and beliefs.

This resource also helpfully suggests that we should acknowledge our own cultural baggage and inherited idolatries before

---

2   Keller, T (2010) *Generous Justice - how God's grace makes us just*, London, Hodder, p141

pronouncing judgement on other seemingly more obvious religious idolatries. We need to be conscious of the associations that people of other religions make between Christianity and the West, imperialism, race, colonialism, wealth and class. These confusions need to be attended to in order to address the combination of envy and loathing with which some other religions view the 'Christian West'.[3] We correct these perceptions when we match up our words and our deeds.

Although it is clear that the issue of idolatry cannot and should not be side-stepped, there is also a recognition that there are more fruitful opportunities to evangelise the 'religious other' than those of secular non-religious belief systems. We should be encouraged by this, and also accept that understanding the nature and cultural assumptions of non-Christian religions is vital. As with the communication of the gospel, gaining a better understanding should be compelled by love. This is a love of God that flows from knowing God's love for us. It's a love for all those made in His image – accompanied by a firm conviction that the greatest act of love is to introduce the lost to our Lord and Saviour Jesus. This is what compels evangelicals to proclaim and live out the gospel. Love must be the fuel of mission and evangelism.

On a practical level this means taking an interest in people's lives, and getting involved practically. It is also likely to mean living among non-Christian faith communities. This intentional building of friendships is what will best enable Christians to assess what those in other religions actually know about Jesus and also what they think about his followers. Often people in

---

3   Pearse, M (2004) *Why the Rest Hates the West: Understanding the Roots of Global Rage*, London, IVP

other religions can confuse Christianity with the prevailing Western secular liberalism/relativism that plagues our society. Without a commitment to bringing understanding by 'loving our neighbours' it is hard to see how evangelicals can bridge the cultural gap for the gospel. In other words, the Church needs to adapt to reach out.

Dialogue is obviously critical for engagement with adherents from other faiths. However, the syncretism of inter-faith ecumenism in which core doctrinal beliefs are compromised is both impractical and dishonourable. Despite what our comfort-seeking society would like to believe, all religions are not equally valid, and all truth claims are not equally true. Contrary to the 'faith sector' language of government policy, religious plurality means diversity, not similitude. It's a fruit salad, not a fruit puree. As the former Chief Rabbi Jonathan Sacks noted, there is dignity in difference.[4]

In relation to theology and belief, it is encouraging that this resource shows how acknowledging and respecting difference can be more successful than seeking the lowest common denominator. As such, the theological framework explored in this resource suggests that an attitude of what could be called 'confident humility' is needed for engagement with people of other religions. This will naturally require features such as hospitality, humanity, friendship and humour to characterise our engagement.

Done with the right motives and tone, a more open and honest premise for engagement is what creates the context

---

4   Sacks, J (2004) *The Dignity of Difference: How to Avoid the Clash of Civilizations*, London, Continuum

for authentic witness. Notwithstanding the gospel imperative, given the proliferation of faith forums and partnerships, the relationships of trust engendered by this approach are likely to support more effective co-belligerence and cooperation on social and political issues of mutual concern. These common endeavours should be encouraged if we are to head off a polarised society and avoid a zero-sum culture war scenario akin to the US. In our own social context in which religion is treated with either indifference or hostility, it is important for religions (and religious leaders) to be seen to be working together for tolerance, social cohesion and the common good. This is especially important given that many religions are concentrated in areas of social deprivation in which a unity of voice and vision among faith leaders can have a powerful effect.

There is a prevailing myth of secular neutrality. The effect of this myth has been to infuse our social and political institutions with either religious illiteracy or a form of default secularism. The result is that today, the project of multiculturalism – whereby assimilating incomer groups to a host culture was not encouraged – is being exposed as failing. It simply doesn't supply the common identity and social cohesion that we all need to be able to live with our deepest differences. Both left and right, and state and market are complicit in this failure because mass migration has been instrumentalised by both the cultural Marxism of Antonio Gramsci and the free-market economics of Milton Freidman. In the vacuum that these secular ideas have created, it is vital that Christians take a lead to provide a positive and inclusive narrative to other faith communities in the UK.

As liberal social elites continue to either neglect or wilfully deny the truth that their many freedoms and securities derive from

Christianity and the Bible, it is important that evangelicals help those in other religions to value the roots as well as the fruits of our cultural blessings. Consequently, fostering a common commitment to religious freedom needs to be a missional priority for Christians in the UK. Evangelicals have a particular stake in this because the gospel is synonymous with freedom. Both personally and corporately, it demands and sustains freedom. The freedoms that the gospel delivers beget more freedoms. Historically, this has informed the development of human rights and civil liberties, thus making religious liberty a foundation for our many other rights and freedoms. Today, secularism has largely divorced freedom from virtue, and in relation to the freedoms we have become accustomed to enjoying in the West, only Christianity can supply the habits of the heart needed for a renewal of a free and civil society.

In light of this, as evangelicals we should not shrink back from playing our part in encouraging a plural society in which everyone has the right to hear and understand the gospel – and to freely accept or reject it. This means that as we engage with other religions it is vitally important that we do so in way that promotes and defends religious freedom for all. There can be no sectional freedoms. We should be calling for justice, not 'just us'.

If religious freedom is at the core of our other freedoms, then the freedom to convert is at the core of religious freedom. Without it there simply is no freedom of religion. As such, it is critical that evangelicals firmly and graciously convey the non-negotiable nature of this freedom to other religions. We should also recognise that, in our evangelism to other religions, 'proselytism' is not, as some secularists would argue, a problem. On the contrary. The religious freedom to preach for conversion is probably one the few signifiers we have as to the depth and health of our liberal democracy. In this sense, being tied to broader freedoms, evangelism can be seen as an act of social justice. All the more reason for us to speak up.[5] Accordingly, if we are serious about defending the freedom to convert, we will also need to accept that we have a responsibility to actively promote it as a right among all faiths.

From the experience of those who have converted from other religions to Christianity, it is clear that, although the Church can be welcoming and loving, the practical implications of the transition can sometimes be missed. The reality is that the Church needs to become a new family for the convert. This can mean going beyond normal Christian pastoral hospitality to provide housing, food, health care and even employment – while always being mindful of the challenges of cultural diversity. The conversion 'blind spot' alluded to in this book represents new challenges to the discipleship deficit in the UK Church.

Today in the UK we have what is described as the 'reverse missionary' movement in which believers from continents historically evangelised by the British are returning the blessing in our own culture. These incomers from Africa, Asia, North and South America and Australasia often bring with them knowledge and experience of dealing with the other religions that we now encounter in the UK. Alongside cultural and linguistic knowledge, they can also offer new perspectives, resources and passion to reach adherents of other religions with the gospel. The phenomenon is most welcome, and the work of the One People Commission of the Evangelical Alliance is a testimony of what is possible through unity for the gospel. It also provides a

---

5   www.greatcommission.co.uk/speak-up

pointer to the future character of the UK Church – a Church of "every tribe, tongue and nation".[6]

Many parts of the world that are dominated by other religions are repressive and hostile to the gospel. To live as a Christian in these places can be dangerous. To share the gospel often comes at a high cost to life and liberty. With so much of the world closed off to the Word of God, perhaps we should be thankful that many from such lands are arriving in the UK? After all, we live in a country where we can share our faith with confidence and impunity. So, the challenge that we face with other religions in the UK, can be seen as an opportunity to reach the world with the good news of salvation in Jesus Christ – right on our doorstep.

6   www.eauk.org/onepeople

# Resources

## Organisations

**The Centre for Muslim-Christian Studies** in Oxford
cmcsoxford.org.uk

**Friends International** friendsinternational.uk

**Global Connections**
globalconnections.org.uk/mission-issues/all

**The Kirby Lang Institute for Christian Ethics.** There is a wealth of material available in their website -
klice.co.uk

**The Lausanne Movement** For a good introduction to the insider Movement and the debate it has generated see
lausanne.org/content/muslim-followers-of-jesus

**Mahabba Network** mahabbanetwork.com

**South Asian Concern** southasianconcern.org

**South Asian Forum of the Evangelical Alliance**
eauk.org/saf  Email: saf@eauk.org

**Theos** - a Christian think tank which believes you can't understand the modern world without understanding religion - theosthinktank.co.uk

# Evangelism, discipleship and training Courses

*Al Massira* ('The Journey') Presents the Christian faith through a chronological overview of the Bible. It centres the Christian faith in its original Middle Eastern context and so is particularly suitable for Muslims from that background. almassira.org

*Alpha* is a series of interactive sessions that freely explore the basics of the Christian faith. alpha.org

*Back to Basics,*
Dave Thurston & Steve Cree, A 7 week course on basic Christian belief and living, The Good Book Company

*Built on the Rock*, Southampton Lighthouse International Church

*Christianity Explored* is based on the Gospel of Mark and so provides an ideal opportunity to learn more about Jesus, His identity and His mission. christianityexplored.org

*Come follow Me* Tim Green, 2014 available at mahabbanetwork.com/prayer/come-follow-me

*Cross and Crescent*, CMS/Faith to Faith, A study course, developed on Islam for Christians. Available from Global Connections - globalconnections.org.uk

*Discover* looks at life issues (with particular relevance to Asians) and the story of the Bible (with focus on the life and teaching of Jesus).
southasianconcern.org/prayer_room/detail/discover/

***Discovering Jesus through Asian Eyes***,
Good Book Company, 2014
Eight session study course with Leaders Guide and
workbook. Based on *Jesus through Asian Eyes: 16 frequently
asked questions*

***East+West***
A course which helps you understand the cultural and
religious background and practices of South Asians, from
basics to more advanced guidelines on communicating with
people of other faiths. It can be run as a one-day course or
series of shorter events.

***Friendship First***
Steve Bell & Tim Green,
An interactive, non-specialist course in six-sessions published
by Interserve UK. It enables Christians to approach their
Muslim friends with confidence by equipping them with the
skill and resources needed to be an effective witness to Jesus
Christ.

***I.D. International Discipleship Course***,
Friends International, 2013

**Jay Smith**For written and video resources by Jay Smith see
debate.org.uk

***Life Explored*** is a new course from Christianity Explored
ministries that introduces people to Jesus through a series of
short films. ceministries.org/Groups/274684/Home/Courses/
Life_Explored/Life_Explored.aspx

***Notes for the Journey: Following Jesus, Staying South
Asian,*** Rasiah, C. and Thomson, Robin, South Asian Concern,
2011

**The Visa Course** is intended for international students (particularly language students), covering the basics of Christian faith in simple language.

**Word of Life** There is a lot of material available at word.org.uk including a multi lingual free course on Jesus for Muslims

## Websites

### The Office of National Statistics
website section on data has a wealth of information ons.gov.uk/ons/index.html

**The Presence and Engagement** website of the Church of England have a facility 'to find out what faiths are present in your parish' - http://presenceandengagement.org.uk

**Aradhna Music** Worship music in a fusion of eastern and western music styles, 'centred around spiritual enlightenment and transformation', building bridges between cultures aradhnamusic.com

**A Baptist Perspective on Interfaith Dialogue** is available at http://baptist.org.uk/Publisher/File.aspx?ID=129959

**Lapido Media** - lapidomedia.com

**The Sanctuary, Birmingham** A church that is Asian in its worship. eastandwest.co.uk/sanctuary.html

The **'Scriptural Reasoning'** movement has its own website - scripturalreasoning.org

**Southampton Lighthouse International Church** provides stories of people who have started to follow Jesus as well as answers to questions about the Christian faith. lighthouseicc.org.uk

# Education resources

The website of the **Transforming Lives** project that existed to promote teaching as a Christian vocation: transforminglives.org.uk

**Prayer Spaces in Schools**
prayerspacesinschools.com/about-us

There are a number of websites that provide material for school assemblies. For example:

**Scripture Union**
scriptureunion.org.uk/YourCommunity/Schools/Resources/AssemblyResources/22367.id

**SPCK** assemblies.org.uk

**Spinnaker** 'A team of committed Christians with links to the mainstream churches within the Christian community. We operate in 14 hubs around South London, Kent, Surrey and West Sussex, supporting primary schools in the delivery of Christian collective worship and religious education.' spinnaker.org.uk/about/who-we-are

For material in the Welsh language see beibl.net

# Information about other religions

## *Buddhism*

Buddhism in the United Kingdom en.wikipedia.org/wiki/
Buddhism_in_the_United_Kingdom

BBC material on British Buddhism
bbc.co.uk/religion/religions/buddhism/history/
britishbuddhism_1.shtml#top

## *Hinduism*

Hinduism in the United Kingdom en.wikipedia.org/wiki/
Hinduism_in_the_United_Kingdom

Hindu Council of UK hinducouncil.net

Hindu Forum of Britain hfb.org.uk/

## *Judaism*

Jews in the UK en.wikipedia.org/wiki/British_Jews

Jews in numbers from the website of the Board of Deputies
bod.org.uk/jewish-facts-info/jews-in-numbers/

## *Islam*

Muslims in the UK en.wikipedia.org/wiki/
Islam_in_the_United_Kingdom

MCB report on the 201 Census mcb.org.uk/wp-content/
uploads/2015/02/MCBCensusReport_2015.pdf

British Muslim Forum britishmuslimforum.co.uk

Muslim Council of Britain [MCB] mcb.org.uk/about-mcb/

## Sikhism

Sikhs in the UK en.wikipedia.org/wiki/
Sikhism_in_the_United_Kingdom

The British Sikh Report 2013 britishsikhreport.org/
wp-content/uploads/2013/06/BSR_2013_FINAL.pdf

# Bibliography

Alexander & Thomson (eds), *Walking the Way of the Cross with our Hindu Friends,* Interserve, Bangalore, 2011.
With accompanying DVD.

Alupoaicei, Marla, *Your Intercultural Marriage,*
Moody Publishers, 2009

Barclay, David, *Making multiculturalism work: enabling practical action accross deep difference,* Theos, 2013

Barnes, L. Philip, *Education, Religion and Diversity: Developing a new model of religious education,* Routledge, 2014

Bartholomew and Moritz, ed., *Christ and Consumerism: A Critical Analysis of the Spirit of the Age,* Carlisle, Paternoster, 2000

Basham, A. L., *The Sacred Cow: The Evolution of Classical Hinduism,* edited by and annotated by Kenneth G Zysk,
Rider, 1989

Bavinck, J. H. *The Church Between the Temple and Mosque, A Study of the Relationship Between the Christian Faith and other Religions,* Grand Rapids, Eerdmans, 1960

Bavinck, J. H., *An Introduction to the Science of Missions,* Philadeplphia, Presbyterian and Reformed Publishing Company, 1960

Bell and Chapman, *Between Naivety and Hostility; Uncovering the best Christian responses to Islam in Britain,* Milton Keynes, Authentic, 2011

Bell, Steve *Gospel for Muslims,* Authentic, 2012

Bell, Steve, *Grace for Muslims?* Authentic, 2006

Bharati, Dayanand, *Living Water and Indian Bowl,*
William Carey Library, 2004

Bhatt, C., 'Dharmo rakshati rakshitah: Hindutva movements in the UK'. *Ethnic and Racial Studies* 23(3) May 2000, pp. 559-93

Blackden, Celia, *Friendship and Exchange with People of Other Faiths: A Context for Witness and Dialogue*, Grove Books

Bluck, Robert, 'Buddhism and Ethnicity in Britain: The 2001 Census Data', *Journal of Global Buddhism* 5 (2004)

Board for Mission and Unity, *Towards a Theology of Interfaith Dialogue*, Church House Publishing, 1995

Bookless, David, *Interfaith Worship and Christian Faith*, Grove Books, 1991

Bowen, Innes *Medina in Birmingham, Najaf in Brent: Inside British Islam,* C, Hurst & Co, 2014

Brockington, John, *Hinduism and Christianity*, Macmillan, London, 1992

Burnett, David *Spirit of Hinduism*, Monarch, 2006

Cooling, Trevor and Margaret, *Grove Education: Distinctively Christian Learning?,* , Grove Books: Cambridge, 2013.

Cooling, Trevor, *Doing God in Education*, Theos, 2010 available at theosthinktank.co.uk/publications/2010/12/02/doing-god-in-education

Chaplin, Jonathan, *'Living with Difference': Time for a Constructive Christian Engagement.* KLICE Comment, Jan. 2016 at tyndalehouse.cmail20.com/t/ViewEmail/r/A912C5F47C55258F2540EF23F30FEDED/D8EB69E1850C72A7C9C291422E3DE149 [Comment on *Living with Difference: Community, Diversity and the Common Good*, the report of the Cambridge-based Woolf Institute's Commission on Religion and Belief in British Public Life (CORAB)]

Chaplin, Jonathan, *Multiculturalism: a Christian retreival*, Theos, 2011

Chaplin, Jonathan, *Talking God: The Legitimacy of Religious public Reasoning*, Theos, 2008

Chapman, Colin, 'Towards a Theology for Inter-Faith Dialogue: A Personal Response' A review of the church report above available at biblicalstudies.org.uk/pdf/churchman/100-02_129.pdf

Chapman, Colin, *The Bible Through Muslim Eyes - and a Christian Response*, Grove Books

Davda, , Suneel Shivdasani, Robin Thomson & Margaret Wardell, *Looking for Directions: towards an Asian spirituality*, South Asian Concern, 2006

Davda, Shivdasani, Thomson & Wardell, *Looking for Directions: towards an Asian spirituality*, South Asian Concern, 2006

Daya Prakash, Acharya, *Fulfilment of the Vedic Pilgrimage in the Lord Jesus Christ*, 2nd edtion, OM Books, 2004

Dowsett, Rose, ed., *Global Mission: Reflections and Case Studies in Contextualization for the Whole Church*, William Carey Library, Pasadena, 2011

Ellul, Jacques, *The New Demons,* London, Mowbrays, 1976

Evangelical Alliance, *Faith and Nation: Report of a Commission of Inquiry to the UK Evangelical Alliance*, 2006

Gamadia, Dr Sam, *Christian Approach to Hinduism*

Gandhi, M *An Autobiography: The story of my Experiments with Truth*, Navijivan, 1927

Gidoomal & Thomson, *A Way of life: Introducing Hinduism*, Hodder, 1997 *(out of print)*

Gidoomal & Wardell *Lions, Princesses, Gurus: Reaching your Sikh Neighbour*, Highland, 1996

Gidoomal & Wardell, *Chapatis for Tea: Reaching your Hindu Neighbour*, Highland, 1994

Gidoomal & Wardell, *Lions, Princesses, Gurus: Reaching your Sikh Neighbour*, Highland, 1996

Gidoomal, Ram *Sari'n' Chips*, Kingsway/SAC, 1993

Goldsmith, Martin, *Islam and Christian Witness*, Authentic Media, 1991

Goudzwaard, Bob, *Idols of our Time*, Downers Grove, InterVarsity Press, 1984

Green with Cooling, Mapping the Field: *A review of the current research evidence on the impact of schools with a Christian ethos,* Theos, 2009 - theosthinktank.co.uk/files/files/Reports/Mappingthefield.pdf

Fuller, C. J. *The Camphor Flame: Popular Hinduism and Society in India*, Princeton University Press, Princeton, 1992

Guptara, Prabhu and Osmaston, Amiel *Yoga - A Christian Option?* Grove Books Ltd, 1987

Hopkins, T. J., *The Hindu Religious Tradition: The Religious Life of Man*, Wadsworth Publishing Co, California, 1971

Husain, Ed *The Islamist: Why I joined radical Islam in Britain, What I saw Inside and why I left*, London: Penguin Books, 2007.

Hussain, Khalad, *Against the Grain*, Xlibris, 2012

Kanitkar and Cole, *Hinduism*: Teach Yourself Books World Faiths, Hodder, 1995

Kateregga & Shenk, *A Muslim and Christian in Dialogue*, Scottdale: Herald Press, 1997

Knott, Kim, *A very short introduction to Hinduism*, Oxford University Press, 1998

Krabill, Shenk and Stutzman, eds, *Anabaptists Meeting Muslims: A Calling for Presence in the Way of Christ*, Scottdale: Herald Press, 2005, pp330-347

Lamb, Christopher, 'Mixed-Faith Marriages: A Case for Care' in Roger Hooker & Christopher Lamb, *Love the Stranger: Ministry in Multi-Faith Areas*, SPCK, 1986

Lewis P., 'Being Muslim and Being British' in Ballard (ed.), *Desh Pardesh* London: Hurst, 1994, pp. 58-87

Mangalwadi, Vishal, *The world of Gurus*: revised edition Cornerstone Press, Chicago, 1992

Maharaj with Hunt, *Death of a Guru*, Hodder & Stoughton, 1978

Mahtani, D and C *Sindhi Journeys of Faith*, May 2010

Mahtani, Deepak & Celia, *Sindhi Journeys of Faith*, 2nd ed. 2011

May, Peter, *Dialogue in Evangelism*, Grove Books

Menski, W., 'Law, religion and South Asians'. Unpublished paper for Symposium 'A Comparative Study of the South Asian Diaspora Religious Experience in Britain, Canada and the USA', SOAS, London, 4-6 November 1996

Moore, Peter C., *Disarming the Secular Gods*, Downers Grove, InterVarsity Press, 1989

Moreau, A. Scott, *Contextialisation in World Missions: Mapping and Assessing Evangelical Models*, Kregel Academic, 2012

Moulin, Daniel, 'What religious students have to tell us about RE', RE Online Thinkpiece: reonline.org.uk/news/thinkpiece-what-religious-students-have-to-tell-us-about-re-dr-daniel-moulin/

Oliver-Dee, Sean, *Religion and Identity: Divided Loyalties?*, Theos 2009

Qureshi, Nabeel, *Seeking Allah, Finding Jesus*, Zondervan, 2014

Raithatha, Manoj, *Filthy Rich: the Property Tycoon who Struck Real Gold*, Monarch Books, 2015

Ramachandra, Vinoth, *Gods that Fail, Modern Idolatry and Christian Mission*, Calisle, Paternoster, 1996

Rasiah, & Thomson, *Notes for the Journey: Following Jesus, Staying South Asian*, South Asian Concern, 2011

Rawlings, Phil, *Engaging with Muslims: Building Cohesion while Seeking Conversion*, Grove Books

Richard, H.L., *Following Jesus in the Hindu Context: N.V.Tilak*, William Carey Library, Pasadena, 1998, 2001

Richard, H.L., *Hinduism*, William Carey Library, Pasadena, 1998, 2001

Richard, H.L., *R.C. Das: Evangelical Prophet for Contextual Christianity*, CISRS/ISPCK, Delhi, 1995, 1999

Ruiter, Bert de, *A Single Hand Cannot Applaud: The value of using the Book of Proverbs in Sharing the Gospel with Muslims*, VTR Publications, 2011

Ruiter, Bert de, *Engaging with Muslims in Europe*, VTR Publications, 2014

Ruiter, Bert de, *Sharing Lives: Overcoming our Fear of Islam*, VTR Publications, 2010

Scott, Basil *God Has No Favourites: The New Testament on First Century Religions*, Primalogue, 2013

Scott, Robert, *'Dear Abdullah': Eight Questions Muslim People ask about Christianity*, IVP, 2011

Schafer Riley, Naomi, *'Til Faith Do us Part*, OUP, 2013

Selby, Pauline, *Persian Springs*, Highland Books, 2001

Sheikh, Bilquis, *I dared to call him Father*, Baker, 1978, 2000

Shelling & Fraser-Smith, *In Love but Worlds Apart*, AuthorHouse 2008

Shortt, John, *Bible-shaped Teaching*, Wipf and Stock, 2014

Smith and Carvill *The Gift of the Stranger: Faith, Hospitality, and Foreign Language Learning*, Wm. B. Eerdmans, 2000.

Smith and Smith, *Teaching and Christian Practices: Reshaping Faith and Learning*, Wm. B. Eerdmans, 2011.

Smith, Alex, A *Christian's Pocket Guide to Buddhism*, Christian Focus Publications, 2009

Smith, Andrew, 'Working with Muslim and Christian Young People' in S.Bell and C Chapman, *Between Naivety and Hostility; uncovering the best Christian responses to Islam in Britain*, Authentic: Milton Keynes, 2011, pp. 203-217.

Smith, Andrew, *Faith, Friendship and Pedagogy: Equipping Christian teenagers for a relevant engagement with Muslim peers*, TH.D. theses, Uni. Of Birmingham, 2007, which is available for downloading from the British Library.

Smith, David, *Learning from the Stranger: Christian Faith and Cultural Diversity*, Wm. B. Eerdmans, 2009

Smith, Jay 'The Case for Polemics' in S. Bell and C. Chapman, *Between Naivety and Hostility*, Milton Keynes: Authentic, 2011, pp. 235-247.

Sookhdeo, Patrick, *A Christian's Pocket Guide to Islam*, Christian Focus Publications, 2010

Spencer, Nick, *"Doing God": A Future for Faith in the Public Square*, Theos 2006

Spencer, Nick, *How to Think about Religious Freedom*, Theos, 2014.

Strange, Daniel *Their Rock is not our Rock: A Theology of Religion*, Nottingham, Apollos, 2014

Sutcliffe, Sally (ed), *Good News for Asians in Britain*, Grove Books Ltd, 1998

Taylor, Jenny, 'After secularism: inner city governance and the new religious discourse', Whitefield Briefing, vol.7 no. 5, Dec. 2002

Taylor, Jenny, *After Secularism: Inner-City Governance and the New Religious Discourse*, London: School of Oriental and African Studies, 2002

Trigg, Roger, *Free to Believe? Religious Freedom in a Liberal Society*, Theos, 2010

*The Church School of the Future Review*, Church of England Archbishop's Council Education Division/The National Society, 2012

Theos, *More than an Educated Guess: Assessing the evidence on faith schools*, Theos, 2013 - theosthinktank.co.uk/research/all-reports?p=2

Thomson, Robin *Changing India: insights from the margin*, BRPC, 2002 (distributed in the UK by South Asian Concern)

Thomson, Robin, *Engaging with Hindus*, Good Book Company, 2014

Thorne, Clive, *Light out of darkness*, Southampton Lighthouse International Church

Viswanathan, Ed, *Am I a Hindu? The Hinduism Primer*, Rupa and Co, Calcutta, 1993

Walter, J. A. *A Long way from Home: A Sociological Exploration of Contemporary Idolatry*, Carlisle, Paternoster, 1979

Wingate, Andrew *The Meeting of Opposites? Hindus and Christians in the West*, SPCK, 2014

Wink, Walter, *Engaging the Powers,* Minneapolis, Fortress Press, 1992

Wink, Walter, *Naming the Powers*, Philadelphia, Fortress Press, 1984

Wink, Walter, *Unmasking the Powers*, Philadelphia, Fortress Press, 1986

Wright, Christopher J. H. *The Mission of God*, Nottingham, IVP, 2006

Zacharias Pieri, *Tablighi Jamaat in Britain (Handy Books for Journalists on Religion in World Affairs)*, Lapido Media, 2012

Zebiri, K., 'Muslim Anti-Secularist Discourse in the Context of Muslim-Christian Relations'. *Islam and Christian-Muslim Relation 9(1)*, 1998, pp. 47-64

Baptist Union of Great Britain, 'Can we participate fully in shared worship?' in *Faith and Society Files: Inter Faith Engagements*, p. 32 available at http://baptist.org.uk/Publisher/File.aspx?ID=111214&view=browser

Baptist Union of Great Britain, *12 Myths of Inter Faith Engagement*, available at: baptist.org.uk/Articles/370647/12_Myths_of.aspx

Gidoomal, Ram, *Coming to Britain: An Immigrant's story*, CTA, distributed by Trinity Vision (DVD)